THE PASTOR'S

Wedding Planner

BY STAN TOLER

BEACON HILL PRESS
OF KANSAS CITY

Copyright 2008
By Stan Toler and Beacon Hill Press of Kansas City

ISBN 978-0-8341-2425-7

Printed in the United States of America

Cover Design: J.R. Caines
Interior Design: Sharon Page

Library of Congress Cataloging-in-Publication Data

Toler, Stan.
  The pastor's wedding planner / Stan Toler.
    p. cm.
  Includes bibliographical references (p.).
  ISBN 978-0-8341-2425-7 (pbk.)
  1. Marriage service. 2. Marriage counseling. 3. Marriage—Religious aspects—Christianity. I. Title.
  BV199.M3T65 2008
  265'.5—dc22

                                 2008038871

10 9 8 7 6 5 4 3 2 1

Contents

Introduction

You lean back in your office chair and grab your coffee cup. It had been pretty much a routine day, until now. The couple in front of you has just popped the question, "Pastor, will you perform our wedding?"

Now what?

You may have been through this process dozens of times before. Or this may be your first wedding. In either case, this manual is a resource for making a couple's wedding day something special. With this manual, you will learn how to guide a couple in planning a ceremony that will bring honor to Christ and affirm their commitment to each other.

But you have an added responsibility. You will guide them in preparing for *marriage,* not just a ceremony. As it's often said, "There is no more lovely, friendly or charming relationship, communion or company, than a good marriage." You have the unique privilege of guiding a couple in making the promise that, in theory, makes two persons one.

In practice, as you may know, the assignment can be difficult. Often, just getting a consensus on a time for the wedding rehearsal can be monumental. The multi-tasking minister needs ready resources that ask the right questions and give the right answers for the meeting of the minds that culminates in the wedding ceremony.

Of course, marriage is more than saying vows or greeting guests. The wedding is just the beginning— but it must be a good beginning. Often, more thought is given to taking a vacation to the coast than to taking that solemn journey down the aisle of a church. It is your job to create an appreciation for the wedding process and to give enough background about marriage to guide their future decisions. You will give a couple the opportunity to focus on the permanent instead of the immediate. You will be God's representative, ready to share biblical truths that often stand against the current ideas of society.

As a pastor, I'm always needing resource materials that are practical and that fit my theology. This is a result of that need. This wedding manual maintains values and beliefs while providing traditional and contemporary helps for the officiating minister. It is a one-stop resource for nearly every part of the wedding ceremony.

With *The Pastor's Wedding Planner,* you will be able to lead the couple through discussions that will heighten their emotional and spiritual awareness. It will give you some options that will ease the job of pronouncing them man and wife, as well as make it all the more meaningful. The manual provides:

- Premarital counseling topics
- Traditional and contemporary vows
- Renewal vows and special ceremonies
- Message outlines
- Scripture readings
- Benediction variations
- Wedding information forms
- Wedding policy sample
- Online resources

In addition to all of these resources, this book contains an emphasis on scriptural holiness as it relates to the marriage relationship. In an age of relativity, God speaks of absolutes. His Word is the *best* marriage manual, and His heart is always open to questions about healing and wholeness. I pray God's anointing on you as you represent the King and His kingdom.

—Stan Toler

1

Why Should I Perform the Wedding?

Maybe you have never stared into the eyes of a moonstruck couple and asked yourself, "Why should I perform their wedding?" Or maybe marriage has become just a part of your job description as a minister. Either case, somewhere along the way most of us have lost the callousness of the "marryin' and buryin'" routine as we have tried to come to grips with the gravity of these sacred ceremonies.

Even more than a funeral, a wedding is of serious import. A funeral honors a life already lived; a wedding heralds a life *to be* lived—a life shared by two people whose future will be inexorably altered by this day's event.

So, why should you marry them?

Because it is God's idea. "For this reason a man will leave his father and mother and be united to his wife, and they will become one flesh" (Gen. 2:24).

Because it models God's faithfulness to His people. "I will betroth you to me forever; I will betroth you in righteousness and justice, in love and compassion. I will betroth you in faithfulness, and you will acknowledge the LORD" (Hos. 2:19-20).

Because Jesus honored it. "And Jesus and his disciples had also been invited to the wedding" (John 2:2).

Because it represents Christ and the Church. "'For this reason a man will leave his father and mother and be united to his wife, and the two will become one flesh.' This is a profound mystery—but I am talking about Christ and the church" (Eph. 5:31-32).

Because it's a good thing. "He who finds a wife finds what is good and receives favor from the LORD" (Prov. 18:22).

Because it passes the faith along. "Has not the LORD made them one? In flesh and spirit they are his. And why one? Because he was seeking godly offspring. So guard yourself in your spirit, and do not break faith with the wife of your youth" (Mal. 2:15).

2

Perfect Love: A Holiness Lifestyle

Someone once described the Bible's view of marriage as the total commitment of the total person for the total life. The idea of a totally committed and loving relationship between a husband and wife is God's idea. God is love, and everything He gives to us comes from His perfect love for us. He is absolutely pure in all of His thoughts and actions toward us.

While God does not demand absolute or human perfection of His creation (a creation that dwells in an imperfect society and is prone to imperfection), His ideal is for us to be perfect in heart—in motive, in intention, and in determination to obey the principles of His Word. We are called to be perfect in our promise to fulfill our marriage vows in a thoughtful and faithful way.

Human hearts that are free from selfishness and filled with the love of God are hearts that can become blended in spiritual, emotional, and physical unity. God made a challenging request of His creation when He called us to holiness: "But just as he who called you is holy, so be holy in all you do; for it is written:

'Be holy, because I am holy'" (1 Pet. 1:15-16). Holiness is a lifestyle that finds its source and supply in God and is modeled by those who love Him—and love each other.

It is only through living holy that we can obtain perfect love. Sound impossible? It's not. Every believer in Christ is called to live a holy life: "God has called us to live holy lives, not impure lives" (1 Thess. 4:7, NLT). And what God calls us to do, He equips us to do: "If we confess our sins, he is faithful and just and will forgive us our sins and purify us from all unrighteousness" (1 John 1:9).

Holiness results from being filled with the Holy Spirit, as Eph. 5:18 reminds us: "Be filled with the Spirit." A heart full of self and selfishness cannot act or react in a loving way. But a heart filled with and controlled by the Spirit of Christ is one that expresses itself in a selfless and sacrificial way. "Since we are living by the Spirit, let us follow the Spirit's leading in every part of our lives" (Gal. 5:25, NLT).

Holiness deals with the root cause of selfish behavior. As the writer of James reminds us, it is our selves that get in the way of what Christ could do through us: "What causes fights and quarrels among you? Don't they come from your desires that battle within you? You want something but don't get it. You kill and covet, but you cannot have what you want. You quarrel and fight. You do not have, because you do not ask

God" (4:1-2). The self-centered, sinful—carnal—heart is prone to have its own way, and thus it neglects the tenderness and compassion that so characterized Christ.

Holiness is revealed in everyday life: "Those who live according to the sinful nature have their minds set on what that nature desires; but those who live in accordance with the Spirit have their minds set on what the Spirit desires" (Rom. 8:5).

Those who seek a holiness lifestyle confess every known sin to God, ask in faith to be filled with the Spirit, and claim the infilling according to the promise of God. As 1 John reminds us, "This is the confidence we have in approaching God: that if we ask anything according to his will, he hears us. And if we know that he hears us—whatever we ask—we know that we have what we asked of him" (5:14-15).

3

Premarital Counseling Topics

You don't even have to drag him to the car. The future bridegroom shows up for the counseling session with a smile just a bit too wide to be natural. He looks as comfy as can be sitting on the couch with a protective arm around his sweet fiancée. We're talking about marriage, and his wedding day is the biggest thing on his personal radar screen. It doesn't hurt a bit to be here today.

That's exactly why premarital counseling is a big deal.

Fast forward fifteen years. Few husbands willingly come to a pastor for marital counseling. No matter the scope of the problem, men perceive the need for a third voice as an admission of failure. *I couldn't work this out on my own. I was inadequate,* they think. For a man, walking through the door of the pastor's office for marital counseling is akin to fumbling the ball on the one-yard line as the buzzer sounds on the clock—it's a situation any man will do his best to avoid.

So, the wedding-planning period is the time to plant seeds of truth that will hopefully remain throughout the marriage. But before the crunch of reality, some vital topics need to be addressed.

Session One: Relationships

Topic: God
Text: Matt. 6:31-33
> Why is God the Center of everything?
>> He created you.
>> He has a purpose for you.
>> He knows your future together.
>> His strength will be there in the tough times.
>> His way is what works.

Topic: How should a couple approach their relationship to God?
Text: Judg. 13:2-18
> They prayed together.
> She included her husband in the revelation.
> The man spoke for and in protection of his wife.

Topic: Parenting
Text: Eph. 6:4; Pss. 128:3; 144:12; 127:4-5; Col. 3:21
> Discuss the possibilities of parenting.
> Determine your attitude about parenting.
> Why are children considered gifts?
> What are your views on disciplining children?

Discuss nurturing and training by having family devotions and family activities.

Discuss this common thought: "That is one thing I've always said my kids would never have to go through."

Topic: In-laws
Text: Ruth 3:5; 4:15-16

Avoid being on the outs with your in-laws.

Decide to honor them—they're here to stay.

Learn their passions and hobbies.

Discover how they were raised.

Appreciate their good qualities.

Never pit your spouse against them.

Never complain to your parents about your spouse.

Session Two: Daily Life

Topic: Handling God's Money
Text: Acts 5:1-10

Discuss God's ownership.

Discuss stewardship.

What are your individual views of the use of money as it relates to shopping? What happens to those views now that you are combining households?

Discuss money managing. Who will handle the money, balance the checkbook, or pay the bills?

What are your views on using a budget? How will you maintain your budget?

Discuss the dangers of credit cards and debt.

Discuss the idea of honoring God with your resources (tithe, generosity, charity, etc.).

Do you ever find yourself thinking this thought: "In our finances, I hope that we . . ."? What are those hopes about your finances?

Topic: Around the House

Text: Gal. 6:1-10

Discuss routines. How do they relate to our personalities?

Discuss the household duties. Will you help each other with those? Why is that important?

Discuss this thought: "In our house, I hope we can . . ." Do you have hopes like those? What are they?

Session Three: Oneness

Topic: Devotions

Text: Acts 18:26; Rom. 16:3; 1 Cor. 16:19

Why are devotions an important aspect of your relationship with God?

How will you handle respecting each other's need for spending that individual time alone with God?

What are the benefits of having devotions as a couple?

Topic: Conflict Resolution
Text: Rom. 12:9-21
>   Discuss conflict.
>> Will conflict happen during your marriage?
>> Is conflict the end of the world?
>   Discuss the process of conflict resolution.
>> Identify the problem.
>> Understand the problem in light of the past.
>> Respect each other's perspective.
>> It's over when it's over.
>   Why is conflict resolution important?

Topic: Sex and Intimacy
Text: 1 Cor. 7:1-7
>   Discuss sex.
>> It is the sealing of the marriage covenant.
>> It is a sacred act designed by God for pleasure and procreation.
>> It is both a privilege and a responsibility.
>   Discuss a woman's perspective of sex.
>> A woman is *relationship*-oriented.
>> Atmosphere and mood are important.
>> Sex drive is *cyclical.*
>> Daily events are important—they affect a woman's desire.

Touch and words are central.

Arousal is gradual.

Discuss a man's perspective of sex.

A man is *physically*-oriented.

Any mood is fine for sex.

Sex drive is *acyclical.*

Visual stimuli and flirting are central.

Arousal is immediate.

Discuss sexual intimacy.

Guard and cherish sexual intimacy—make time for it.

Read books on intimacy.

Attend a marriage seminar.

Openly discuss your concerns.

4

Planning the Wedding Ceremony: Seven Ways to Avoid the Wedding Day Blues

Good planning is always important, but especially in planning a wedding. Everything must be taken into account when planning a wedding—from the seating of guests to the flower girl's mind-set. The minister is the prophet, counselor, floor director, and sometimes referee, and has the opportunity to lead the flock to the wedding promised land.

Covering a few important bases may not prevent a bride or groom from hyperventilating, but it will keep the train on the track long enough to pronounce the marriage and introduce the couple to those who are waiting for a slice of wedding cake.

To keep the wedding day in control and the chaos to a minimum, here are seven important principles for avoiding the wedding day blues:*

W—Welcome advice from a wedding coordinator. Experienced counsel doesn't cost; it pays.

E—Enjoy the process. Treat wedding details as ways to express your love.

D—Don't wait until the last moment. Planning ahead helps to alleviate anxiety and irritations.

D—Discipline yourself against overspending; set and practice budget guidelines.

I—Invite married friends to recommend hired services, such as musicians, sound experts, videographers, caterers, or decorators.

N—Never take sole ownership of the wedding; weddings are for couples.

G—Give instructions to the wedding participants. Don't assume anything.

---

*These seven principles can also be found in Appendix F.

The Wedding Ceremony

Vows: Traditional

Traditional Vows

Introduction

The marriage ceremony is both a very solemn and a very delightful occasion. In a marriage ceremony, two loving hearts make a solemn vow before the Lord God to blend their dreams, their affections, and their very lives into one family. But it is also a delight as the joys of a dating relationship are fulfilled in the hopes of an exciting and rewarding life together.

_____ and _____, you have so met on this day that was ordained by God before the foundation of the world. The eternal part of your relationship will find its deepest meaning in the Word of God, for it tenderly portrays the first marriage in a garden called Eden. In Genesis 2 we read,

> The LORD God said, "It is not good for the man to be alone. I will make a helper suitable for him." . . . Then the LORD God made a woman from the rib he had taken out of the man, and he brought her to the man. The man said, "This is now bone of my bones and flesh of my flesh; she shall be called 'woman,' for she was taken out of man." For this reason a man will leave his father and mother and be united to his wife, and they will become one flesh *(vv. 18, 22-24).*

The first of Jesus' miracles was performed at a wedding in Cana of Galilee. His presence there sanctioned the marriage relationship and provided a dimension that made it both a happy and a blessed occasion. His presence in your lives will add that same dynamic, and you will be blessed as you seek first His kingdom and His righteousness.

Declaration of Intent

_____ and _____, do you so commit your lives each to the other in the sight of God and this gathering of your friends and loved ones? If so, answer, "We do."

_____ *(groom)*, will you have this woman to be your wife, to live together in the counsel of God in the holy relationship of marriage? Will you love her, comfort her, honor her, and keep her in sickness and in health, and forsaking all others, keep yourself only unto her so long as you both shall live? If so, answer, "I will."

_____ *(bride)*, will you have this man to be your husband, to live together in the counsel of God in the holy relationship of marriage? Will you love him, comfort him, honor him, and keep him in sickness and in health, and forsaking all others, keep yourself only unto him so long as you both shall live? If so, answer, "I will."

Giving of the Bride

As an act of blessing on the home that will be established this day, who gives this woman to be married to this man?

"Her mother and I."
Couple joins hands.

Scripture Reading

God's Word says, "Therefore, as God's chosen people, holy and dearly loved, clothe yourselves with compassion, kindness, humility, gentleness and patience. Bear with each other and forgive whatever grievances you may have against one another. Forgive as the Lord forgave you. And over all these virtues put on love, which binds them all together in perfect unity" (Col. 3:12-14).

Wedding Vows

In keeping with the instruction of the Word of God, then, now make your vows each to the other.

_____ *(groom),* please repeat this vow to your bride:

Before God, I, _____, take you,
_____, to be my wife, to have and to hold
from this day forward, in times of plenty and in
times of want, in sickness and in health, to love with
a faithful love, until death alone separates us.

_____ *(bride)*, will you likewise repeat your vow to your groom?

Before God, I, _____, take you, _____, to be my husband, to have and to hold from this day forward, in times of plenty and in times of want, in sickness and in health, to love with a faithful love, until death alone separates us.

Giving of Rings

In a sense, the wedding ring typifies your marriage relationship. Its golden purity symbolizes your pledge to be faithful in thought and deed to your partner. Its unending circumference symbolizes your vow of allegiance for time and eternity. It is placed on that finger, which, as legend declares, is linked to the heart. So may you now seal your vow by giving and receiving the wedding rings.

_____ *(groom)*, what symbol do you have of your wedding vow?

"This ring."

_____ *(groom)*, place this on your bride's ring finger and repeat after me:

This ring I give to you, in token and pledge of our constant faith and abiding love.

_____ *(bride)*, what token do you have of your wedding vow?

"This ring."

_____ *(bride),* place this on your groom's ring finger and repeat after me:

This ring I give to you, in token and pledge of our constant faith and abiding love.

Scripture Reading

"Love is patient, love is kind. It does not envy, it does not boast, it is not proud. It is not rude, it is not self-seeking, it is not easily angered, it keeps no record of wrongs. Love does not delight in evil but rejoices with the truth. It always protects, always trusts, always hopes, always perseveres" (1 Cor. 13:4-7).

Pastoral Prayer

Having declared your vows and sealed them with the wedding rings, let us ask God's blessing on the home you are now to establish.

God of love who expressed faithfulness and sacrifice in the person of the Lord Jesus Christ, I ask Your blessing on these hearts who establish their home on this day. May they seek Your wisdom for their every decision, Your strength for their every adversity, and Your presence for every single day of their lives. May their laughter spring from Your eternal joy, and may they be conscious that their tears fall upon Your loving heart. Make them un-

usually strong in their faithfulness to each other. Give them grace to stand against the fleeting attitudes of the world and grace to stand upon the eternal values of Your Word. I pray that their vows may be more than words— make them a way of life as they cautiously begin this journey together. Let Christ be served as their Lord and the Holy Spirit sought as their Guide. In honor of Your name and in recognition of Your love, we pray. Amen.

Pronouncement

Forasmuch as _____ and _____ have agreed in holy wedlock, have witnessed the same before God and this gathering of their loved ones and friends, and have pledged their faith each to the other and declared the same by joining hands, I pronounce that they are husband and wife together, in the name of the Father, and of the Son, and of the Holy Spirit. Those whom God joins together, let no one separate.

You may kiss your bride.

Benediction

"May the grace of the Lord Jesus Christ, and the love of God, and the fellowship of the Holy Spirit be with you" [2 Cor. 13:14] as you so live together in this world, that in the world to come you may have life everlasting. Amen.

Introduction of Couple

And now it is my privilege to introduce to you, Mr. and Mrs. _____.

Traditional Vows with Unity Candle
(Option 1)

Introduction

The marriage ceremony is both a very solemn and a very delightful occasion. In a marriage ceremony, two loving hearts make a solemn vow before the Lord God to blend their dreams, their affections, and their very lives into one family. But it is also a delight as the joys of a dating relationship are fulfilled in the hopes of an exciting and rewarding life together.

_____ and _____, you have so met on this day that was ordained by God before the foundation of the world. The eternal part of your relationship will find its deepest meaning in the Word of God, for it tenderly portrays the first marriage in a garden called Eden. In Genesis 2 we read,

> The LORD God said, "It is not good for the man to be alone. I will make a helper suitable for him." . . . Then the LORD God made a woman from the rib he had taken out of the man, and he brought her to the man. The man said, "This is now bone of my bones and flesh of my flesh; she shall be called 'woman,' for she was taken out of man." For this reason a man will leave his father and mother and be united to his wife, and they will become one flesh *(vv. 18, 22-24)*.

The first of Jesus' miracles was performed at a wedding in Cana of Galilee. His presence there sanctioned the marriage relationship and provided a dimension that made it both a happy and a blessed occasion. His presence in your lives will add that same dynamic, and you will be blessed as you seek first His kingdom and His righteousness.

Declaration of Intent

_____ and _____, do you so commit your lives each to the other in the sight of God and this gathering of your friends and loved ones? If so, answer, "We do."

_____ *(groom)*, will you have this woman to be your wife, to live together in the counsel of God in the holy relationship of marriage? Will you love her, comfort her, honor her, and keep her in sickness and in health, and forsaking all others, keep yourself only unto her so long as you both shall live? If so, answer, "I will."

_____ *(bride)*, will you have this man to be your husband, to live together in the counsel of God in the holy relationship of marriage? Will you love him, comfort him, honor him, and keep him in sickness and in health, and forsaking all others, keep yourself only unto him so long as you both shall live? If so, answer, "I will."

Giving of the Bride

As an act of blessing on the home that will be established this day, who gives this woman to be married to this man?

"Her mother and I."

Couple joins hands.

Scripture Reading

God's Word says, "Therefore, as God's chosen people, holy and dearly loved, clothe yourselves with compassion, kindness, humility, gentleness and patience. Bear with each other and forgive whatever grievances you may have against one another. Forgive as the Lord forgave you. And over all these virtues put on love, which binds them all together in perfect unity" (Col. 3:12-14).

Wedding Vows

In keeping with the instruction of the Word of God, then, now make your vows each to the other.

_____ *(groom),* please repeat this vow to your bride:

Before God, I, _____, take you, _____, to be my wife, to have and to hold from this day forward, in times of plenty and in times of want, in sickness and in health, to love with a faithful love, until death alone separates us.

_____ *(bride)*, will you likewise repeat your vow to your groom?

Before God, I, _____, take you, _____, to be my husband, to have and to hold from this day forward, in times of plenty and in times of want, in sickness and in health, to love with a faithful love, until death alone separates us.

Giving of Rings

In a sense, the wedding ring typifies your marriage relationship. Its golden purity symbolizes your pledge to be faithful in thought and deed to your partner. Its unending circumference symbolizes your vow of allegiance for time and eternity. It is placed on that finger, which, as legend declares, is linked to the heart. So may you now seal your vow by giving and receiving the wedding rings.

_____ *(groom)*, what symbol do you have of your wedding vow?

"This ring."

_____ *(groom)*, place this on your bride's ring finger and repeat after me:

This ring I give to you, in token and pledge of our constant faith and abiding love.

_____ *(bride),* what token do you have of your wedding vow?

"This ring."

_____ *(bride),* place this on your groom's ring finger and repeat after me:

This ring I give to you, in token and pledge of our constant faith and abiding love.

Scripture Reading

"Love is patient, love is kind. It does not envy, it does not boast, it is not proud. It is not rude, it is not self-seeking, it is not easily angered, it keeps no record of wrongs. Love does not delight in evil but rejoices with the truth. It always protects, always trusts, always hopes, always perseveres" (1 Cor. 13:4-7).

Unity Candle Ceremony

_____ and _____, your vows are further symbolized by the lighting of the unity candle. Its outer candles remind us of your individual lives, created perfectly by God as unique expressions of His love and made in His spiritual image. The center candle reminds us of the merger of those individual lives and of a common faith in the Lord.

As you bring the flames of your separate candles together in unity of heart and unity of faith, you acknowledge that your lives are one. And with the psalmist you declare, "Unless the LORD builds the house, its builders labor in vain" (Ps. 127:1).

Pastoral Prayer

Having declared your vows and your common faith in the Lord Jesus Christ, let us ask His blessing on the home you are now to establish.

God of love who expressed faithfulness and sacrifice in the person of the Lord Jesus Christ, I ask Your blessing on these hearts who establish their home on this day. May they seek Your wisdom for their every decision, Your strength for their every adversity, and Your presence for every single day of their lives. May their laughter spring from Your eternal joy, and may they be conscious that their tears fall upon Your loving heart. Make them unusually strong in their faithfulness to each other. Give them grace to stand against the fleeting attitudes of the world and grace to stand upon the eternal values of Your Word. I pray that their vows may be more than words—make them a way of life as they cautiously begin this journey together. Let Christ be served as their Lord and the Holy Spirit sought as their Guide. In honor of Your name and in recognition of Your love, we pray. Amen.

Pronouncement

Forasmuch as _____ and _____ have

agreed in holy wedlock, have witnessed the same before God and this gathering of their loved ones and friends, and have pledged their faith each to the other and declared the same by joining hands, I pronounce that they are husband and wife together, in the name of the Father, and of the Son, and of the Holy Spirit. Those whom God joins together, let no one separate.

You may kiss your bride.

Benediction

"May the grace of the Lord Jesus Christ, and the love of God, and the fellowship of the Holy Spirit be with you" [2 Cor. 13:14] as you so live together in this world, that in the world to come, you may have life everlasting. Amen.

Introduction of Couple

And now it is my privilege to introduce to you, Mr. and Mrs. _____.

Traditional Vows with Unity Candle
(Option 2)

Introduction

Dearly beloved, we are gathered together in the sight of God and in the presence of these witnesses to join together this man and this woman in holy matrimony, which is an honorable estate instituted of God and signifies unto us the mystical union that exists between Christ and His Church. It is a holy estate that Christ adorned and beautified with His presence in Cana of Galilee and that the apostle Paul commended as honorable among all men. It is not, therefore, to be entered into unadvisedly; but reverently, discreetly, and in the fear of God.

Charge to the Bride and Groom

_____ and _____, I require and charge you both, as you stand in the presence of God, to remember that love and loyalty alone will avail as the foundation of a happy and enduring home. There are no other human ties more tender and no other vows more sacred than those you now assume. If these solemn vows be faithfully kept, and if steadfastly you endeavor to do the will of your Heavenly Father, your life will be full of joy, and the home you are establishing will abide in peace.

Declaration of Intent

_____ *(groom)*, will you have this woman to be your wedded wife, to live together after God's ordinance in the holy estate of matrimony? Will you love her, comfort her, honor her, and keep her in sickness and in health, and forsaking all others, keep yourself only unto her so long as you both shall live?

"I will."

_____ *(bride)*, will you have this man to be your wedded husband, to live together after God's ordinance in the holy estate of matrimony? Will you love him, comfort him, honor him, and keep him in sickness and in health, and forsaking all others, keep yourself only unto him so long as you both shall live?

"I will."

Giving of the Bride

Who gives this woman to be married to this man?

"Her mother and I."

Couple joins hands.

Wedding Vows

I, _____ *(groom)*, take you, _____ *(bride)*, to be my wedded wife, to have and to hold from this day forward, for better or for worse, for richer or for poorer, in sickness and in health, to love and to cherish, till death do us part.

I, _____ *(bride),* take you, _____
(groom), to be my wedded husband, to have and to
hold from this day forward, for better or for worse, for
richer or for poorer, in sickness and in health, to love
and to cherish, till death do us part.

Giving of Rings

Though small in size, this ring is very large in signifi-
cance. Made of precious metal, it reminds us that love
is neither cheap nor common. In fact, love is costly.
Made in a circle, its design symbolizes that love must
never come to an end. As you wear these rings, may
they be a constant reminder of these glad promises
you make today.

Place the ring on the ring finger of the left hand and
repeat after me:

> *Groom:* I give you this ring as a symbol of my vow;
> with all that I am and all that I have, I honor you.
> In the name of the Father, and of the Son, and of
> the Holy Spirit.

> *Bride:* I give you this ring as a symbol of my vow;
> with all that I am and all that I have, I honor you.
> In the name of the Father, and of the Son, and of
> the Holy Spirit.

Unity Candle Ceremony

The unity candle is a symbol of the merging of your two lives into a union of mutual submission and unselfish love. As you bring the flames together to light the larger candle, let it be a witness to all that your first thoughts will be for each other. Let it be a testimony that as you share your joys and sorrows, your successes and failures, and your mutual desire to find God's plan for your lives, the flame of true love will burn brightly and the light of God's love will shine undiminished through your marriage.

Pronouncement of Couple

Forasmuch as _____ and _____ have consented together in holy wedlock, have witnessed the same before God and this company, and thereto have pledged their faith each to the other and have declared the same by joining hands, I pronounce that they are husband and wife together, in the name of the Father, and of the Son, and of the Holy Spirit.

You may kiss your bride.

Introduction of Couple

And now it is my privilege to introduce to you for the very first time, Mr. and Mrs. _____.

Traditional Vows with Unity Candle and Communion

Introduction

The marriage ceremony is both a very solemn and a very delightful occasion. In a marriage ceremony, two loving hearts make a solemn vow before the Lord God to blend their dreams, their affections, and their very lives into one family. But it is also a delight as the joys of a dating relationship are fulfilled in the hopes of an exciting and rewarding life together.

_____ and _____, you have so met on this day that was ordained by God before the foundation of the world. The eternal part of your relationship will find its deepest meaning in the Word of God, for it tenderly portrays the first marriage in a garden called Eden. In Genesis 2 we read,

> The LORD God said, "It is not good for the man to be alone. I will make a helper suitable for him." . . . Then the LORD God made a woman from the rib he had taken out of the man, and he brought her to the man. The man said, "This is now bone of my bones and flesh of my flesh; she shall be called 'woman,' for she was taken out of man." For this reason a man will leave his father and mother and

be united to his wife, and they will become one flesh *(vv. 18, 22-24)*.

The first of Jesus' miracles was performed at a wedding in Cana of Galilee. His presence there sanctioned the marriage relationship and provided a dimension that made it both a happy and a blessed occasion. His presence in your lives will add that same dynamic, and you will be blessed as you seek first His kingdom and His righteousness.

Declaration of Intent

_____ and _____, do you so commit your lives each to the other in the sight of God and this gathering of your friends and loved ones? If so, answer, "We do."

_____ *(groom)*, will you have this woman to be your wife, to live together in the counsel of God in the holy relationship of marriage? Will you love her, comfort her, honor her, and keep her in sickness and in health, and forsaking all others, keep yourself only unto her so long as you both shall live? If so, answer, "I will."

_____ *(bride)*, will you have this man to be your husband, to live together in the counsel of God in the holy relationship of marriage? Will you love him, comfort him, honor him, and keep him in sickness and in health, and forsaking all others, keep yourself only unto him so long as you both shall live? If so, answer, "I will."

Giving of the Bride

As an act of blessing on the home that will be established this day, who gives this woman to be married to this man?

"Her mother and I."

Couple joins hands.

Scripture Reading

God's Word says, "Therefore, as God's chosen people, holy and dearly loved, clothe yourselves with compassion, kindness, humility, gentleness and patience. Bear with each other and forgive whatever grievances you may have against one another. Forgive as the Lord forgave you. And over all these virtues put on love, which binds them all together in perfect unity" (Col. 3:12-14).

Wedding Vows

In keeping with the instruction of the Word of God, then, now make your vows each to the other.

_____ *(groom),* please repeat this vow to your bride:

Before God, I, _____, take you,
_____, to be my wife, to have and to hold
from this day forward, in times of plenty and in
times of want, in sickness and in health, to love
with a faithful love, until death alone separates us.

_____ *(bride),* will you likewise repeat your
vow to your groom?

Before God, I, _____, take you,
_____, to be my husband, to have and to
hold from this day forward, in times of plenty and
in times of want, in sickness and in health, to love
with a faithful love, until death alone separates us.

Giving of Rings

In a sense, the wedding ring typifies your marriage relationship. Its golden purity symbolizes your pledge to
be faithful in thought and deed to your partner. Its
unending circumference symbolizes your vow of allegiance for time and eternity. It is placed on that finger,
which, as legend declares, is linked to the heart. So
may you now seal your vow by giving and receiving
the wedding rings.

_____ *(groom),* what symbol do you have of
your wedding vow?

"This ring."

_____ *(groom),* place this on your bride's ring finger, and repeat after me:

This ring I give to you, in token and pledge of our constant faith and abiding love.

_____ *(bride),* what token do you have of your wedding vow?

"This ring."

_____ *(bride),* place this on your groom's ring finger and repeat after me:

This ring I give to you, in token and pledge of our constant faith and abiding love.

Scripture Reading

"Love is patient, love is kind. It does not envy, it does not boast, it is not proud. It is not rude, it is not self-seeking, it is not easily angered, it keeps no record of wrongs. Love does not delight in evil but rejoices with the truth. It always protects, always trusts, always hopes, always perseveres" (1 Cor. 13:4-7).

Unity Candle Ceremony

_____ and _____, your vows are further symbolized by the lighting of the unity candle. Its outer candles remind us of your individual lives, created perfectly by God as unique expressions of His love and made in His spiritual image. The center candle reminds us of the merger of those individual lives and of a common faith in the Lord.

As you bring the flames of your separate candles together in unity of heart and unity of faith, you acknowledge that your lives are one. And with the psalmist you declare, "Unless the LORD builds the house, its builders labor in vain" (Ps. 127:1).

Communion Ceremony

As an expression of their common faith and a declaration that Christ is the center of their home,
_____ and _____ have requested that they share in the observance of the Lord's Supper.

"The Lord Jesus, on the night he was betrayed, took bread, and when he had given thanks, he broke it and said, 'This is my body, which is for you; do this in remembrance of me'" (1 Cor. 11:23b-24).

Serving of Bread: Take and eat this in remembrance that Christ died for you, and feed on Him in your heart by faith, with thanksgiving.

"In the same way, after supper he took the cup, saying, 'This cup is the new covenant in my blood; do this, whenever you drink it, in remembrance of me.' For whenever you eat this bread and drink this cup, you proclaim the Lord's death until he comes" (1 Cor. 11:25-26).

Serving the Cup: Drink this in remembrance that Christ's blood was shed for you and be thankful.

Pastoral Prayer

Having declared your vows and your common faith in the Lord Jesus Christ, let us ask His blessing on the home you are now to establish.

God of love who expressed faithfulness and sacrifice in the person of the Lord Jesus Christ, I ask Your blessing on these hearts who establish their home on this day. May they seek Your wisdom for their every decision, Your strength for their every adversity, and Your presence for every single day of their lives. May their laughter spring from Your eternal joy, and may they be conscious that their tears fall upon Your loving heart. Make them unusually strong in their faithfulness to each other. Give them grace to stand against the fleeting attitudes of the world and grace to stand upon the eternal values of Your Word. I pray that their vows may be more than words—make them a way of life as they cautiously begin this journey together. Let Christ be served as their Lord and the Holy Spirit sought as their Guide. In honor of Your name and in recognition of Your love, we pray. Amen.

Pronouncement

Forasmuch as _____ and _____ have agreed in holy wedlock, have witnessed the same before God and this gathering of their loved ones and friends, and have pledged their faith each to the other and declared the same by joining hands, I pronounce that they are husband and wife together, in the name of the Father, and of the Son, and of the Holy Spirit. Those whom God joins together, let no one separate.

You may kiss your bride.

Benediction

"May the grace of the Lord Jesus Christ, and the love of God, and the fellowship of the Holy Spirit be with you" [2 Cor. 13:14] as you so live together in this world, that in the world to come, you may have life everlasting. Amen.

Introduction of Couple

And now it is my privilege to introduce to you, Mr. and Mrs. _____.

Traditional Vows with
Step-Family Vows

Introduction

The marriage ceremony is both a very solemn and a very delightful occasion. In a marriage ceremony, two loving hearts make a solemn vow before the Lord God to blend their dreams, their affections, and their very lives into one family. But it is also a delight as the joys of a dating relationship are fulfilled in the hopes of an exciting and rewarding life together.

_____ and _____, you have so met on this day that was ordained by God before the foundation of the world. The eternal part of your relationship will find its deepest meaning in the Word of God, for it tenderly portrays the first marriage in a garden called Eden. In Genesis 2 we read,

> The LORD God said, "It is not good for the man to be alone. I will make a helper suitable for him." . . . Then the LORD God made a woman from the rib he had taken out of the man, and he brought her to the man. The man said, "This is now bone of my bones and flesh of my flesh; she shall be called 'woman,' for she was taken out of man." For this reason a man will leave his father and mother and

be united to his wife, and they will become one flesh *(vv. 18, 22-24)*.

The first of Jesus' miracles was performed at a wedding in Cana of Galilee. His presence there sanctioned the marriage relationship and provided a dimension that made it both a happy and a blessed occasion. His presence in your lives will add that same dynamic, and you will be blessed as you seek first His kingdom and His righteousness.

Declaration of Intent

_____ and _____, do you so commit your lives each to the other in the sight of God and this gathering of your friends and loved ones? If so, answer, "We do."

_____ *(groom)*, will you have this woman to be your wife, to live together in the counsel of God in the holy relationship of marriage? Will you love her, comfort her, honor her, and keep her in sickness and in health, and forsaking all others, keep yourself only unto her so long as you both shall live? If so, answer, "I will."

_____ *(bride)*, will you have this man to be your husband, to live together in the counsel of God in the holy relationship of marriage? Will you love him, comfort him, honor him, and keep him in sickness and in health, and forsaking all others, keep yourself only unto him so long as you both shall live? If so, answer, "I will."

Giving of the Bride

As an act of blessing on the home that will be established this day, who gives this woman to be married to this man?

"Her mother and I."

Couple joins hands.

Scripture Reading

God's Word says, "Therefore, as God's chosen people, holy and dearly loved, clothe yourselves with compassion, kindness, humility, gentleness and patience. Bear with each other and forgive whatever grievances you may have against one another. Forgive as the Lord forgave you. And over all these virtues put on love, which binds them all together in perfect unity" (Col. 3:12-14).

Wedding Vows

In keeping with the instruction of the Word of God, then, now make your vows each to the other.

_____ *(groom)*, please repeat this vow to your bride:

Before God, I, _____, take you,
_____, to be my wife, to have and to hold
from this day forward, in times of plenty and in
times of want, in sickness and in health, to love
with a faithful love, until death alone separates us.

_____ *(bride),* will you likewise repeat your
vow to your groom?

Before God, I, _____, take you,
_____, to be my husband, to have and to
hold from this day forward, in times of plenty and
in times of want, in sickness and in health, to love
with a faithful love, until death alone separates us.

Giving of Rings

In a sense, the wedding ring typifies your marriage relationship. Its golden purity symbolizes your pledge to
be faithful in thought and deed to your partner. Its
unending circumference symbolizes your vow of allegiance for time and eternity. It is placed on that finger,
which, as legend declares, is linked to the heart. So
may you now seal your vow by giving and receiving
the wedding rings.

_____ *(groom),* what symbol do you have of
your wedding vow?

"This ring."

_____ *(groom),* place this on your bride's ring finger and repeat after me:

This ring I give to you, in token and pledge of our constant faith and abiding love.

_____ *(bride),* what token do you have of your wedding vow?

"This ring."

_____ *(bride),* place this on your groom's ring finger and repeat after me:

This ring I give to you, in token and pledge of our constant faith and abiding love.

Scripture Reading

"Love is patient, love is kind. It does not envy, it does not boast, it is not proud. It is not rude, it is not self-seeking, it is not easily angered, it keeps no record of wrongs. Love does not delight in evil but rejoices with the truth. It always protects, always trusts, always hopes, always perseveres" (1 Cor. 13:4-7).

Step-Family Vows

The marriage of _____ and _____ not only includes a blending of hearts but also a blending of families. Each member of this home will enjoy a unique and wonderful relationship with the others. The merging of your lives into one family will at times be both awkward and awesome. Yet within the borders of blessing provided by a loving family, there will be an opportunity for common expression and common personal growth—and common faith.

You have heard your parents vow to make their home a place of harmony and love. Will you also promise before God to do your part to make this home a place where Christ is the center and where warmth and acceptance prevail?

    Children: "We will."

Will you seek by example to make your home a place of gentleness, harmony, and support?

    Children: "We will."

Pastoral Prayer

Having declared your vows and sealed them with the wedding rings, let us ask God's blessing on the home you are now to establish.

> *God of love who expressed faithfulness and sacrifice in the person of the Lord Jesus Christ, I ask Your blessing on these hearts who establish their home on this day. May they seek Your wisdom for their every decision, Your strength for their every adversity, and Your presence for every single day of their lives. May their laughter spring from Your eternal joy, and may they*

be conscious that their tears fall upon Your loving heart. Make them unusually strong in their faithfulness to each other. Give them grace to stand against the fleeting attitudes of the world and grace to stand upon the eternal values of Your Word. I pray that their vows may be more than words—make them a way of life as they cautiously begin this journey together. Let Christ be served as their Lord and the Holy Spirit sought as their Guide. In honor of Your name and in recognition of Your love, we pray. Amen.

Pronouncement

Forasmuch as _____ and _____ have agreed in holy wedlock, have witnessed the same before God and this gathering of their loved ones and friends, and have pledged their faith each to the other and declared the same by joining hands, I pronounce that they are husband and wife together, in the name of the Father, and of the Son, and of the Holy Spirit. Those whom God joins together, let no one separate.

You may kiss your bride.

Benediction

"May the grace of the Lord Jesus Christ, and the love of God, and the fellowship of the Holy Spirit be with you" [2 Cor. 13:14] as you so live together in this world, that in the world to come you may have life everlasting. Amen.

Introduction of Couple

And now it is my privilege to introduce to you, Mr. and Mrs. _____.

Traditional Vows with Vows Written by the Couple

Introduction

The marriage ceremony is both a very solemn and a very delightful occasion. In a marriage ceremony, two loving hearts make a solemn vow before the Lord God to blend their dreams, their affections, and their very lives into one family. But it is also a delight as the joys of a dating relationship are fulfilled in the hopes of an exciting and rewarding life together.

_____ and _____, you have so met on this day that was ordained by God before the foundation of the world. The eternal part of your relationship will find its deepest meaning in the Word of God, for it tenderly portrays the first marriage in a garden called Eden. In Genesis 2 we read,

> The LORD God said, "It is not good for the man to be alone. I will make a helper suitable for him." . . . Then the LORD God made a woman from the rib he had taken out of the man, and he brought her to the man. The man said, "This is now bone of my bones and flesh of my flesh; she shall be called 'woman,' for she was taken out of man." For this reason a man will leave his father and mother and

be united to his wife, and they will become one flesh *(vv. 18, 22-24)*.

The first of Jesus' miracles was performed at a wedding in Cana of Galilee. His presence there sanctioned the marriage relationship and provided a dimension that made it both a happy and a blessed occasion. His presence in your lives will add that same dynamic, and you will be blessed as you seek first His kingdom and His righteousness.

Declaration of Intent

_____ and _____, do you so commit your lives each to the other in the sight of God and this gathering of your friends and loved ones? If so, answer, "We do."

_____ *(groom),* will you have this woman to be your wife, to live together in the counsel of God in the holy relationship of marriage? Will you love her, comfort her, honor her, and keep her in sickness and in health, and forsaking all others, keep yourself only unto her so long as you both shall live? If so, answer, "I will."

_____ *(bride),* will you have this man to be your husband, to live together in the counsel of God in the holy relationship of marriage? Will you love him, comfort him, honor him, and keep him in sickness and in health, and forsaking all others, keep yourself only unto him so long as you both shall live? If so, answer, "I will."

Giving of the Bride

As an act of blessing on the home that will be established this day, who gives this woman to be married to this man?

"Her mother and I."
Couple joins hands.

Scripture Reading

God's Word says, "Therefore, as God's chosen people, holy and dearly loved, clothe yourselves with compassion, kindness, humility, gentleness and patience. Bear with each other and forgive whatever grievances you may have against one another. Forgive as the Lord forgave you. And over all these virtues put on love, which binds them all together in perfect unity" (Col. 3:12-14).

Wedding Vows

In keeping with the instruction of the Word of God, then, now make your vows each to the other.

_____ *(groom),* please share your vows to your bride.

Groom recites vows.

_____ *(bride)*, will you likewise share your vows to your groom?

Bride recites vows.

Giving of Rings

In a sense, the wedding ring typifies your marriage relationship. Its golden purity symbolizes your pledge to be faithful in thought and deed to your partner. Its unending circumference symbolizes your vow of allegiance for time and eternity. It is placed on that finger, which, as legend declares, is linked to the heart. So may you now seal your vow by giving and receiving the wedding rings.

_____ *(groom)*, what symbol do you have of your wedding vow?
   "This ring."

_____ *(groom)*, place this on your bride's ring finger and repeat after me:
   This ring I give to you, in token and pledge of our constant faith and abiding love.

_____ *(bride)*, what token do you have of your wedding vow?
   "This ring."

_____ *(bride)*, place this on your groom's ring finger and repeat after me:

This ring I give to you, in token and pledge of our constant faith and abiding love.

Scripture Reading

"Love is patient, love is kind. It does not envy, it does not boast, it is not proud. It is not rude, it is not self-seeking, it is not easily angered, it keeps no record of wrongs. Love does not delight in evil but rejoices with the truth. It always protects, always trusts, always hopes, always perseveres" (1 Cor. 13:4-7).

Pastoral Prayer

Having declared your vows and sealed them with the wedding ring, let us ask God's blessing on the home you are now to establish.

God of love who expressed faithfulness and sacrifice in the person of the Lord Jesus Christ, I ask Your blessing on these hearts who establish their home on this day. May they seek Your wisdom for their every decision, Your strength for their every adversity, and Your presence for every single day of their lives. May their laughter spring from Your eternal joy, and may they be conscious that their tears fall upon Your loving heart. Make them un-usually strong in their faithfulness to each other. Give them grace to stand against the fleeting attitudes of the world and grace to stand upon the eternal values of Your Word. I pray that their vows may be more than words—

make them a way of life as they cautiously begin this journey together. Let Christ be served as their Lord and the Holy Spirit sought as their Guide. In honor of Your name and in recognition of Your love, we pray. Amen.

Pronouncement

Forasmuch as _____ and _____ have agreed in holy wedlock, have witnessed the same before God and this gathering of their loved ones and friends, and have pledged their faith each to the other and declared the same by joining hands, I pronounce that they are husband and wife together, in the name of the Father, and of the Son, and of the Holy Spirit. Those whom God joins together, let no one separate.

You may kiss your bride.

Benediction

"May the grace of the Lord Jesus Christ, and the love of God, and the fellowship of the Holy Spirit be with you" [2 Cor. 13:14] as you so live together in this world, that in the world to come you may have life everlasting. Amen.

Introduction of Couple

And now it is my privilege to introduce to you Mr. and Mrs. _____.

Traditional Vows
(Brief)

Introduction

The marriage ceremony is both a very solemn and a very delightful occasion. In a marriage ceremony, two loving hearts make a solemn vow before the Lord God to blend their dreams, their affections, and their very lives into one family. But it is also a delight as the joys of a dating relationship are fulfilled in the hopes of an exciting and rewarding life together.

_____ and _____, you have so met on this day that was ordained by God before the foundation of the world.

The first of Jesus' miracles was performed at a wedding in Cana of Galilee. His presence there sanctioned the marriage relationship and provided a dimension that made it both a happy and a blessed occasion. His presence in your lives will add that same dynamic, and you will be blessed as you seek first His kingdom and His righteousness.

Declaration of Intent

_____ and _____, do you so commit your lives each to the other in the sight of God and this gathering of your friends and loved ones? If so, answer, "We do."

_____ *(groom),* will you have this woman to be your wife, to live together in the counsel of God in the holy relationship of marriage? Will you love her, comfort her, honor her, and keep her in sickness and in health, and forsaking all others, keep yourself only unto her so long as you both shall live? If so, answer, "I will."

_____ *(bride),* will you have this man to be your husband, to live together in the counsel of God in the holy relationship of marriage? Will you love him, comfort him, honor him, and keep him in sickness and in health, and forsaking all others, keep yourself only unto him so long as you both shall live? If so, answer, "I will."

Giving of the Bride

As an act of blessing on the home that will be established this day, who gives this woman to be married to this man?

"Her mother and I."
Couple joins hands.

Scripture Reading

God's Word says, "Therefore, as God's chosen people, holy and dearly loved, clothe yourselves with compassion, kindness, humility, gentleness and patience. Bear with each other and forgive whatever grievances you may have against one another. Forgive as the Lord forgave you. And over all these virtues put on love, which binds them all together in perfect unity" (Col. 3:12-14).

Wedding Vows

In keeping with the instruction of the Word of God, then, now make your vows each to the other.

_____ *(groom),* please repeat this vow to your bride:

> Before God, I, _____, take you, _____, to be my wife, to have and to hold from this day forward, in times of plenty and in times of want, in sickness and in health, to love with a faithful love, until death alone separates us.

_____ *(bride),* will you likewise repeat your vow to your groom?

> Before God, I, _____, take you, _____, to be my husband, to have and to hold from this day forward, in times of plenty and

in times of want, in sickness and in health, to love with a faithful love, until death alone separates us.

Giving of Rings

_____ *(groom),* what symbol do you have of your wedding vow?
>   "This ring."

_____ *(groom),* place this on your bride's ring finger and repeat after me:
>   This ring I give to you, in token and pledge of our constant faith and abiding love.

_____ *(bride),* what token do you have of your wedding vow?
>   "This ring."

_____ *(bride),* place this on your groom's ring finger and repeat after me:
>   This ring I give to you, in token and pledge of our constant faith and abiding love.

Pastoral Prayer

Having declared your vows and sealed them with the wedding ring, let us ask God's blessing on the home you are now to establish.

God of love who expressed faithfulness and sacrifice in the person of the Lord Jesus Christ, I ask Your blessing on these hearts who establish their home on this day. May they seek Your wisdom for their every decision, Your strength for their every adversity, and Your presence for every single day of their lives. May their laughter spring from Your eternal joy, and may they be conscious that their tears fall upon Your loving heart. Make them unusually strong in their faithfulness to each other. Give them grace to stand against the fleeting attitudes of the world and grace to stand upon the eternal values of Your Word. I pray that their vows may be more than words— make them a way of life as they cautiously begin this journey together. Let Christ be served as their Lord and the Holy Spirit sought as their Guide. In honor of Your name and in recognition of Your love, we pray. Amen.

Pronouncement

Forasmuch as _____ and _____ have agreed in holy wedlock, have witnessed the same before God and this gathering of their loved ones and friends, and have pledged their faith each to the other and declared the same by joining hands, I pronounce that they are husband and wife together, in the name of the Father, and of the Son, and of the Holy Spirit. Those whom God joins together, let no one separate.

You may kiss your bride.

Benediction

"May the grace of the Lord Jesus Christ, and the love of God, and the fellowship of the Holy Spirit be with you" [2 Cor. 13:14] as you so live together in this world, that in the world to come you may have life everlasting. Amen.

Introduction of Couple

And now it is my privilege to introduce to you, Mr. and Mrs. _____.

Vows: Contemporary

Contemporary Vows

Introduction

Thank you for sharing this wonderful day with
_____ and _____. The love they have
found in each other will be celebrated in a brief ceremony, but it will be lived out in words and deeds of
affirmation and affection from this day forward. We
rejoice with these two people who found each other
from all others in the world and who will soon pledge
to commit themselves to be one. Their marriage will
not only celebrate their uniqueness but also celebrate
their collective faith in God whose holy Word taught
us its meaning.

At the dawn of time, the Lord God said to His creation,

> "It is not good for the man to be alone. I will make
> a helper who is just right for him." . . . So the
> Lord God caused the man to fall into a deep
> sleep. While the man slept, the Lord God took
> out one of the man's ribs and closed up the open-
> ing. Then the Lord God made a woman from the
> rib, and he brought her to the man. "At last!" the
> man exclaimed. "This one is bone from my bone,
> and flesh from my flesh! She will be called
> 'woman,' because she was taken from 'man.'" This

explains why a man leaves his father and mother
and is joined to his wife, and the two are united
into one *(Gen. 2:18, 21-24, NLT).*

In the New Testament, Jesus Christ pronounced His
blessing on marriage by His attendance at a wedding
in Cana. In fact, He performed His first miracle at
that wedding. His presence made the difference then,
and His presence will make a difference now.

When Christ is first in your lives, His grace will be
your source and supply. When Christ is first in your
lives, His mighty power will be your strength. You will
see that the closer you both move toward Him, the
closer you will be to each other. As you seek to walk
with Him in holiness, you will model His spirit and
truth in your marriage.

Declaration of Intent

_____ and _____, will you make your
vows of faith and faithfulness to each other?

  "We will."

_____ *(groom),* will you have this woman to be
your wife, to love her with God's love and provide for
her with God's supply? Will you seek to be her best
friend, her most admiring lover, and her dearest companion?

"I will."

_____ *(bride),* will you have this man to be your husband, to love him with God's love and provide for him with God's supply? Will you seek to be his best friend, his most admiring lover, and his dearest companion?

"I will."

Giving of the Bride

As a symbol of love and blessing, who gives this woman to be married to this man?

"Her mother and I."
Couple joins hands.

Scripture Reading

The Word of God says, "Give honor to marriage, and remain faithful to one another in marriage" (Heb. 13:4, NLT).

Wedding Vows

God brought you together in a unique way and in His unique timing. Will you now pledge to honor this gift of His love by making your vows to each other?

_____ *(groom),* please make this vow to your bride:

Before God, I, _____, take you,

_____, to be the one that completes my earthly life. I vow to be faithful to you. I will be with you in good times and in difficult times. I will share my life with you. I will believe in you and affirm you. Mine will be your hand to hold and your shoulder to lean upon. I will care for you, both now and forever.

_____ *(bride),* please make your vow to your groom:

Before God, I, _____, take you, _____, to be the one that completes my earthly life. I vow to be faithful to you. I will be with you in good times and in difficult times. I will share my life with you. I will believe in you and affirm you. Mine will be your hand to hold and your shoulder to lean upon. I will care for you, both now and forever.

Giving of Rings

The wedding ring is so much more than precious metal; it is a symbol of valuable promises. In biblical times the seal of the king was fixed to a letter to prove that it was genuine and personal. It was a visible mark of the sender's faithfulness, and it was received in the same spirit. In a similar sense, the golden purity of your wedding rings symbolizes the purity of your promises. Its unending circumference represents your vow of allegiance for time and eternity.

Please place the wedding ring on the ring finger and repeat after me:

Groom: This ring I give to you as a promise of my constant faith and abiding love.

Bride: This ring I give to you as a promise of my constant faith and abiding love.

Scripture Reading

"Love is patient and kind. Love is not jealous or boastful or proud or rude. It does not demand its own way. It is not irritable, and it keeps no record of being wronged. It does not rejoice about injustice but rejoices whenever the truth wins out. Love never gives up, never loses faith, is always hopeful, and endures through every circumstance" (1 Cor. 13:4-7, NLT).

Pronouncement

On the basis of the love and faithfulness that you have expressed today, by the authority given me as a minister of the gospel, and in accordance with the State of _____, I declare that you are husband and wife, in the name of the Father, and of the Son, and of the Holy Spirit.

You may kiss your bride.

Benediction

"May the grace of the Lord Jesus Christ, and the love of God, and the fellowship of the Holy Spirit be with you" [2 C or. 13:14] as you so live together in this world, that in the world to come you may have life everlasting. Amen.

Introduction of Couple

It is now my privilege to introduce to you, Mr. and Mrs. _____.

Contemporary Vows with Unity Candle

Introduction

Thank you for sharing this wonderful day with
_____ and _____. The love they have
found in each other will be celebrated in a brief ceremony, but it will be lived out in words and deeds of
affirmation and affection from this day forward. We
rejoice with these two people who found each other
from all others in the world and who will soon pledge
to commit themselves to be one. Their marriage will
not only celebrate their uniqueness but also celebrate
their collective faith in God whose holy Word taught
us its meaning.

At the dawn of time, the Lord God said to His creation,

> "It is not good for the man to be alone. I will make
> a helper who is just right for him." . . . So the
> LORD God caused the man to fall into a deep
> sleep. While the man slept, the LORD God took
> out one of the man's ribs and closed up the open-
> ing. Then the LORD God made a woman from the
> rib, and he brought her to the man. "At last!" the
> man exclaimed. "This one is bone from my bone,

and flesh from my flesh! She will be called 'woman,' because she was taken from 'man.'" This explains why a man leaves his father and mother and is joined to his wife, and the two are united into one *(Gen. 2:18, 21-24, NLT)*.

In the New Testament, Jesus Christ pronounced His blessing on marriage by His attendance at a wedding in Cana. In fact, He performed His first miracle at that wedding. His presence made the difference then, and His presence will make a difference now.

When Christ is first in your lives, His grace will be your source and supply. When Christ is first in your lives, His mighty power will be your strength. You will see that the closer you both move toward Him, the closer you will be to each other. As you seek to walk with Him in holiness, you will model His spirit and truth in your marriage.

Declaration of Intent

_____ and _____, will you make your vows of faith and faithfulness to each other?

"We will."

_____ *(groom)*, will you have this woman to be your wife, to love her with God's love and provide for her with God's supply? Will you seek to be her best friend, her most admiring lover, and her dearest companion?

"I will."

_____ *(bride),* will you have this man to be your husband, to love him with God's love and provide for him with God's supply? Will you seek to be his best friend, his most admiring lover, and his dearest companion?

"I will."

Giving of the Bride

As a symbol of love and blessing, who gives this woman to be married to this man?

"Her mother and I."
Couple joins hands.

Scripture Reading

The Word of God says, "Give honor to marriage, and remain faithful to one another in marriage" (Heb. 13:4, NLT).

Wedding Vows

God brought you together in a unique way and in His unique timing. Will you now pledge to honor this gift of His love by making your vows to each other?

_____ *(groom),* please make this vow to your bride:

Before God, I, _____, take you,
_____, to be the one that completes my
earthly life. I vow to be faithful to you. I will be
with you in good times and in difficult times. I
will share my life with you. I will believe in you
and affirm you. Mine will be your hand to hold
and your shoulder to lean upon. I will care for you,
both now and forever.

_____ *(bride),* please make this vow to your
groom:

Before God, I, _____, take you,
_____, to be the one that completes my
earthly life. I vow to be faithful to you. I will be
with you in good times and in difficult times. I
will share my life with you. I will believe in you
and affirm you. Mine will be your hand to hold
and your shoulder to lean upon. I will care for you,
both now and forever.

Giving of Rings

The wedding ring is so much more than precious
metal; it is a symbol of valuable promises. In biblical
times the seal of the king was fixed to a letter to prove
that it was genuine and personal. It was a visible mark
of the sender's faithfulness, and it was received in the
same spirit. In a similar sense, the golden purity of
your wedding rings symbolizes the purity of your

promises. Its unending circumference represents your vow of allegiance for time and eternity.

Please place the wedding ring on the ring finger and repeat after me:

> *Groom:* This ring I give to you as a promise of my constant faith and abiding love.

> *Bride:* This ring I give to you as a promise of my constant faith and abiding love.

Scripture Reading

"Love is patient and kind. Love is not jealous or boastful or proud or rude. It does not demand its own way. It is not irritable, and it keeps no record of being wronged. It does not rejoice about injustice but rejoices whenever the truth wins out. Love never gives up, never loses faith, is always hopeful, and endures through every circumstance" (1 Cor. 13:4-7, NLT).

Unity Candle

_____ and _____, your vows are further symbolized by the lighting of the unity candle. Its outer candles remind us of your individual lives, created perfectly by God as unique expressions of His love and made in His spiritual image. The center candle reminds us of the merger of those individual lives and of a common faith in the Lord.

As you bring the flames of your separate candles together in unity of heart and in unity of faith, you acknowledge that your lives are one. And with the psalmist you declare, "Unless the LORD builds the house, its builders labor in vain" (Ps. 127:1).

Pronouncement

On the basis of the love and faithfulness that you have expressed today, by the authority given me as a minister of the gospel, and in accordance with the State of _____, I declare that you are husband and wife, in the name of the Father, and of the Son, and of the Holy Spirit.

You may kiss your bride.

Benediction

"May the grace of the Lord Jesus Christ, and the love of God, and the fellowship of the Holy Spirit be with you" [2 Cor. 13:14] as you so live together in this world, that in the world to come you may have life everlasting. Amen.

Introduction of Couple

It is now my privilege to introduce to you, Mr. and Mrs. _____.

Contemporary Vows with
Unity Candle and Communion

Introduction

Thank you for sharing this wonderful day with
_____ and _____. The love they have
found in each other will be celebrated in a brief ceremony, but it will be lived out in words and deeds of
affirmation and affection from this day forward. We
rejoice with these two people who found each other
from all others in the world and who will soon pledge
to commit themselves to be one. Their marriage will
not only celebrate their uniqueness but also celebrate
their collective faith in God whose holy Word taught
us its meaning.

At the dawn of time, the Lord God said to His creation,

> "It is not good for the man to be alone. I will make
> a helper who is just right for him." . . . So the
> LORD God caused the man to fall into a deep
> sleep. While the man slept, the LORD God took
> out one of the man's ribs and closed up the open-
> ing. Then the LORD God made a woman from the
> rib, and he brought her to the man. "At last!" the
> man exclaimed. "This one is bone from my bone,

and flesh from my flesh! She will be called
'woman,' because she was taken from 'man.'" This
explains why a man leaves his father and mother
and is joined to his wife, and the two are united
into one *(Gen. 2:18, 21-24, NLT)*.

In the New Testament, Jesus Christ pronounced His
blessing on marriage by His attendance at a wedding
in Cana. In fact, He performed His first miracle at
that wedding. His presence made the difference then,
and His presence will make a difference now.

When Christ is first in your lives, His grace will be
your source and supply. When Christ is first in your
lives, His mighty power will be your strength. You will
see that the closer you both move toward Him, the
closer you will be to each other. As you seek to walk
with Him in holiness, you will model His spirit and
truth in your marriage.

Declaration of Intent

_____ and _____, will you make your
vows of faith and faithfulness to each other?
    "We will."

_____ *(groom),* will you have this woman to be
your wife, to love her with God's love and provide for
her with God's supply? Will you seek to be her best

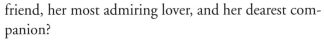

friend, her most admiring lover, and her dearest companion?

"I will."

_____ *(bride),* will you have this man to be your husband, to love him with God's love and provide for him with God's supply? Will you seek to be his best friend, his most admiring lover, and his dearest companion?

"I will."

Giving of the Bride

As a symbol of love and blessing, who gives this woman to be married to this man?

"Her mother and I."
Couple joins hands.

Scripture Reading

The Word of God says, "Give honor to marriage, and remain faithful to one another in marriage" (Heb. 13:4, NLT).

Wedding Vows

God brought you together in a unique way and in His unique timing. Will you now pledge to honor this gift of His love by making your vows to each other?

_____ *(groom),* please make this vow to your bride:

Before God, I, _____, take you,
_____, to be the one that completes my
earthly life. I vow to be faithful to you. I will be
with you in good times and in difficult times. I
will share my life with you. I will believe in you
and affirm you. Mine will be your hand to hold
and your shoulder to lean upon. I will care for you,
both now and forever.

_____ *(bride)*, please make your vow to your
groom:
Before God, I, _____, take you,
_____, to be the one that completes my
earthly life. I vow to be faithful to you. I will be
with you in good times and in difficult times. I
will share my life with you. I will believe in you
and affirm you. Mine will be your hand to hold
and your shoulder to lean upon. I will care for you,
both now and forever.

Giving of Rings

The wedding ring is so much more than precious
metal; it is a symbol of valuable promises. In biblical
times the seal of the king was fixed to a letter to prove
that it was genuine and personal. It was a visible mark
of the sender's faithfulness, and it was received in the
same spirit. In a similar sense, the golden purity of
your wedding rings symbolizes the purity of your

promises. Its unending circumference represents your vow of allegiance for time and eternity.

Please place the wedding ring on the ring finger and repeat after me:

Groom: This ring I give to you as a promise of my constant faith and abiding love.

Bride: This ring I give to you as a promise of my constant faith and abiding love.

Scripture Reading

"Love is patient and kind. Love is not jealous or boastful or proud or rude. It does not demand its own way. It is not irritable, and it keeps no record of being wronged. It does not rejoice about injustice but rejoices whenever the truth wins out. Love never gives up, never loses faith, is always hopeful, and endures through every circumstance" (1 Cor. 13:4-7, NLT).

Unity Candle

_____ and _____, your vows are further symbolized by the lighting of the unity candle. Its outer candles remind us of your individual lives, created perfectly by God as unique expressions of His love and made in His spiritual image. The center candle reminds us of the merger of those individual lives and of a common faith in the Lord.

As you bring the flames of your separate candles together in unity of heart and in unity of faith, you acknowledge that your lives are one. And with the psalmist you declare, "Unless the LORD builds the house, its builders labor in vain" (Ps. 127:1).

Communion Ceremony

As an expression of their common faith and a declaration that Christ is the center of their home, _____ and _____ have requested that they share in the observance of the Lord's Supper.

"The Lord Jesus, on the night he was betrayed, took bread, and when he had given thanks, he broke it and said, 'This is my body, which is for you; do this in remembrance of me'" (1 Cor. 11:23*b*-24).

Serving of Bread: Take and eat this in remembrance that Christ died for you, and feed on Him in your heart by faith, with thanksgiving.

"In the same way, after supper he took the cup, saying, 'This cup is the new covenant in my blood; do this, whenever you drink it, in remembrance of me.' For whenever you eat this bread and drink this cup, you proclaim the Lord's death until he comes" (1 Cor. 11:25-26).

Serving the Cup: Drink this in remembrance that Christ's blood was shed for you and be thankful.

Pronouncement

On the basis of the love and faithfulness that you have expressed today, by the authority given me as a minister of the gospel, and in accordance with the State of _____, I declare that you are husband and wife, in the name of the Father, and of the Son, and of the Holy Spirit.

You may kiss your bride.

Benediction

"May the grace of the Lord Jesus Christ, and the love of God, and the fellowship of the Holy Spirit be with you" [2 Cor. 13:14] as you so live together in this world, that in the world to come you may have life everlasting. Amen.

Introduction of Couple

It is now my privilege to introduce to you, Mr. and Mrs. _____.

Special Wedding Ceremonies

Renewal of Marriage Vows

Introduction

As friends and family members of _____ and _____, you have been invited to witness the renewal of their wedding vows. Marriage was established by God as a covenant of companionship and mutual support. The wedding ceremony is a personal affirmation of that covenant and is the beginning of the marriage process of uniting unique lives with unique personalities, tastes, wants, and needs.

This time of renewal is a public witness to God's faithfulness to the couple and a time for the couple to declare their continuing dependence on Him. The vows they first made are as sacred now as they were on that first wedding day. Only God knows the courage and commitment that has brought this couple to this day. And only the couple knows how their faith in each other, and their faith in God, has led them to this place in time.

Declaration of Intent

_____ and _____, will you now reaffirm the covenant you first made before God? Will you determine to spend the remainder of your lives in a loving and caring companionship? Will you renew your support and affirmation of your spouse, depending on the wisdom of God and the love that He so beautifully displayed by His life and death?

"We will."

Wedding Vows

With marriage as the framework, God symbolizes restoration and renewal in His Word to Israel: "I will make you my wife forever, showing you righteousness and justice, unfailing love and compassion" (Hos. 2:19, NLT). Fairness, faithfulness, compassion—these are the covenants of a successful marriage at any stage of the marriage relationship. The renewal of your vows will reflect those same covenants.

_____ *(husband)*, will you renew your vows to your wife as you repeat after me?

> _____, in love and faithfulness I renew my vow to be your companion. I will care for you when you are in need and I will rejoice with you in plenty. For the rest of my days on earth, I will cherish you with God's love and be sensitive to you with the wisdom of His Holy Spirit.

_____ *(wife)*, will you renew your vows to your husband as you repeat after me?

> _____, in love and faithfulness I renew my vow to be your companion. I will care for you

when you are in need and I will rejoice with you in plenty. For the rest of my days on earth, I will cherish you with God's love and be sensitive to you with the wisdom of His Holy Spirit.

Scripture Reading

God's Word says, "Therefore, as God's chosen people, holy and dearly loved, clothe yourselves with compassion, kindness, humility, gentleness and patience. Bear with each other and forgive whatever grievances you may have against one another. Forgive as the Lord forgave you. And over all these virtues put on love, which binds them all together in perfect unity" (Col. 3:12-14).

Pastoral Prayer

Let us ask God's blessing on these two hearts that have made their vows anew.

God of love who expressed faithfulness and sacrifice in the person of the Lord Jesus Christ, I ask Your blessing on the words and actions of this day. May the renewal of these vows reflect a faith in each other and a faith in You. May they seek Your wisdom for their every decision, Your strength for their every adversity, and Your presence for every single day of their lives. May their laughter spring from Your eternal joy, and may they be conscious that their tears fall upon Your loving heart. Give them grace to stand against the enemies of their heart and home, and grace to stand upon the eternal values of Your Word. I pray that their vows may be more than words—make them a way of life. Let Christ be served as their Lord and the Holy Spirit sought as their Guide. In honor of Your name and in recognition of Your love, we pray. Amen.

Pronouncement

We celebrate this sacred moment and the renewal of the vows that first made these two as one. As a minister of the Word of God, I declare that with renewed faith and resolve, they are husband and wife.

You may kiss your bride.

Benediction

Now may "the peace of God, which transcends all understanding, . . . guard your hearts and your minds in Christ Jesus" [Phil. 4:7]. Amen.

Renewal of Marriage Vows
25th Wedding Anniversary

Introduction

As friends and family members of _____ and
_____, you have been invited to witness the renewal of their wedding vows on this silver anniversary
of their wedding. Twenty-five years ago, God blessed
these two hearts in a celebration of marriage. It was a
covenant of companionship and mutual support.
Many years have passed since that day, but the abiding
commitment that made them one has brought them to
this day of renewal and remembrance. Their journey
has been one of unique circumstances and unique
blessings. We will learn from them as we make our
own vows, and we will look to them as those who have
found grace and favor in the eyes of God.

This time of renewal is a public witness to God's
faithfulness to the couple and a time for the couple to
declare their continuing dependence on Him. The
vows they first made are as sacred now as they were on
that first wedding day. Only God knows the courage
and commitment that has brought this couple to this
day. And only the couple knows how their faith in
each other, and their faith in God, has led them to
this place in time.

Declaration of Intent

_____ and _____, will you now reaffirm the covenant you first made before God? Will you determine to spend the remainder of your lives in a loving and caring companionship? Will you renew your support and affirmation of your spouse, depending on the wisdom of God and the love that He so beautifully displayed by His life and death?

"We will."

Wedding Vows

With marriage as the framework, God symbolizes restoration and renewal in His Word to Israel: "I will make you my wife forever, showing you righteousness and justice, unfailing love and compassion" (Hos. 2:19, NLT). Fairness, faithfulness, compassion—these are the covenants of a successful marriage at any stage of the marriage relationship. The renewal of your vows will reflect those same covenants.

_____ (husband), will you renew your vows to your wife as you repeat after me?

_____, in love and faithfulness I renew my vow to be your companion. I will care for you when you are in need and I will rejoice with you in plenty. For the rest of my days on earth, I will cherish you with God's love and be sensitive to you with the wisdom of His Holy Spirit.

_____ *(wife)*, will you renew your vows to your husband as you repeat after me?

_____, in love and faithfulness I renew my vow to be your companion. I will care for you when you are in need and I will rejoice with you in plenty. For the rest of my days on earth, I will cherish you with God's love and be sensitive to you with the wisdom of His Holy Spirit.

Scripture Reading

God's Word says, "Therefore, as God's chosen people, holy and dearly loved, clothe yourselves with compassion, kindness, humility, gentleness and patience. Bear with each other and forgive whatever grievances you may have against one another. Forgive as the Lord forgave you. And over all these virtues put on love, which binds them all together in perfect unity" (Col. 3:12-14).

Pastoral Prayer

Let us ask God's blessing on these two hearts that have made their vows anew.

God of love who expressed faithfulness and sacrifice in the person of the Lord Jesus Christ, I ask Your blessing on the words and actions of this day. May the renewal of these vows reflect a faith in each other and a faith in You. May they seek Your wisdom for their every decision, Your strength for their every adversity, and Your presence for every single day of their lives. May their laughter spring from Your eternal joy, and may they be conscious that their tears fall upon Your loving heart. Give them grace to stand against the enemies of their heart and home, and grace to stand upon the eternal values of Your Word. I pray that their vows may be more than words—make them a way of life. Let Christ be served as their Lord and the Holy Spirit sought as their Guide. In honor of Your name and in recognition of Your love, we pray. Amen.

Pronouncement

We celebrate this sacred moment and the renewal of the vows that first made these two as one. As a minister of the Word of God, I declare that with renewed faith and resolve, they are husband and wife.

You may kiss your bride.

Benediction

Now may "the peace of God, which transcends all understanding, . . . guard your hearts and your minds in Christ Jesus" [Phil. 4:7]. Amen.

Renewal of Marriage Vows
50th Wedding Anniversary

Introduction

As friends and family members of _____ and
_____, you have been invited to witness the renewal of their wedding vows on this golden anniversary of their wedding. Fifty years ago, God blessed these two hearts in a celebration of marriage. It was a covenant of companionship and mutual support. Many years have passed since that day, but the abiding commitment that made them one has brought them to this day of renewal and remembrance. Their journey has been one of unique circumstances and unique blessings. We will learn from them as we make our own vows, and we will look to them as those who have found grace and favor in the eyes of God.

This time of renewal is a public witness to God's faithfulness to the couple and a time for the couple to declare their continuing dependence on Him. The vows they first made are as sacred now as they were on that first wedding day. Only God knows the courage and commitment that has brought this couple to this day. And only the couple knows how their faith in each other, and their faith in God, has led them to this place in time.

Declaration of Intent

_____ and _____, will you now reaffirm the covenant you first made before God? Will you determine to spend the remainder of your lives in a loving and caring companionship? Will you renew your support and affirmation of your spouse, depending on the wisdom of God and the love that He so beautifully displayed by His life and death?

"We will."

Wedding Vows

With marriage as the framework, God symbolizes restoration and renewal in His Word to Israel: "I will make you my wife forever, showing you righteousness and justice, unfailing love and compassion" (Hos. 2:19, NLT). Fairness, faithfulness, compassion—these are the covenants of a successful marriage at any stage of the marriage relationship. The renewal of your vows will reflect those same covenants.

_____ (husband), will you renew your vows to your wife as you repeat after me:

_____, in love and faithfulness I renew my vow to be your companion. I will care for you when you are in need and I will rejoice with you in plenty. For the rest of my days on earth, I will cherish you with God's love and be sensitive to you with the wisdom of His Holy Spirit.

_____ *(wife),* will you renew your vows to your husband as you repeat after me:

_____, in love and faithfulness I renew my vow to be your companion. I will care for you when you are in need and I will rejoice with you in plenty. For the rest of my days on earth, I will cherish you with God's love and be sensitive to you with the wisdom of His Holy Spirit.

Scripture Reading

God's Word says, "Therefore, as God's chosen people, holy and dearly loved, clothe yourselves with compassion, kindness, humility, gentleness and patience. Bear with each other and forgive whatever grievances you may have against one another. Forgive as the Lord forgave you. And over all these virtues put on love, which binds them all together in perfect unity" (Col. 3:12-14).

Pastoral Prayer

Let us ask God's blessing on these two hearts that have made their vows anew.

God of love who expressed faithfulness and sacrifice in the person of the Lord Jesus Christ, I ask Your blessing on the words and actions of this day. May the renewal of these vows reflect a faith in each other and a faith in You. May they seek Your wisdom for their every decision, Your strength for their every adversity, and Your presence for every single day of their lives. May their laughter spring from Your eternal joy, and may they be conscious that their tears fall upon Your loving heart. Give them grace to stand against the enemies of their heart and home, and grace to stand upon the eternal values of Your Word. I pray that their vows may be more than words—make them a way of life. Let Christ be served as their Lord and the Holy Spirit sought as their Guide. In honor of Your name and in recognition of Your love, we pray. Amen.

Pronouncement

We celebrate this sacred moment and the renewal of the vows that first made these two as one. As a minister of the Word of God, I declare that with renewed faith and resolve, they are husband and wife.

You may kiss your bride.

Benediction

Now may "the peace of God, which transcends all understanding, . . . guard your hearts and your minds in Christ Jesus" [Phil. 4:7]. Amen.

The Wedding Message

Sermon Outlines

The Ten Commandments of Marriage

Text: Matt. 22:37-39

You are being married according to the laws of the state, but there are even higher laws to consider: the laws of God's kingdom.

God's laws are practical truths that are given for our protection, health, and spiritual growth. Apply them to your marriage and you will always be glad you did.

1. Thou shalt keep the lines of communication open.

Text: "Let your conversation be always full of grace" (Col. 4:6).

> The Bible tells us to speak the truth in love, but it also encourages us to speak the truth with compassion and mercy.
>
> "Don't be a stranger" is more than an expression; it is an important ingredient for your marriage.
>
> Learn to know each other by communicating with each other.
>
> Be best friends.

2. Thou shalt learn to compromise.

Text: "Let us therefore make every effort to do what leads to peace" (Rom. 14:19).

Marriage is more than a relationship; it is a partnership. It is two hearts relying on Spirit-led wisdom in a cooperative effort to make decisions that will be mutually beneficial and Christ-honoring.

3. Thou shalt not take each other for granted.

Text: "There are different kinds of gifts, but the same Spirit" (1 Cor. 12:4).

Marriage is a celebration of uniqueness. It is two people with different gifts, abilities, values, and strengths utilizing their individual gifts in the power of the Holy Spirit.

4. Thou shalt keep romance alive.

Text: "Husbands, in the same way be considerate as you live with your wives" (1 Pet. 3:7).

Be affectionate and caring.

Make time for romance.

Tell each other, "I love you."

5. Thou shalt not worship material goods.

Text: "Be content with what you have" (Heb. 13:5).

The things you will treasure most cannot be bought or sold. They are the eternal qualities of your lives and your relationship.

6. Thou shalt be thankful.

Text: "Let the peace of Christ rule in your hearts, since as members of one body you were called to peace. And be thankful" (Col. 3:15).

You will never be too busy to be polite.

Consideration for each other includes saying, "Thank you."

7. Thou shalt not be disrespectful.

Text: "In humility consider others better than yourselves" (Phil. 2:3).

God gave you to each other to support and to affirm each other.

Respect each other as God's highest creation.

8. Thou shalt be accountable.

Text: "Confess your sins to each other and pray for each other so that you may be healed" (James 5:16).

Trust is an important factor in successful marriages.

Develop openness and confidentiality with each other.

9. Thou shalt not bear a grudge.

Text: "Forgive as the Lord forgave you" (Col. 3:13).

Harbored resentments create spiritual and emotional wounds. Learn to ask—and receive—forgiveness.

10. Thou shalt be an encourager.

Text: "Encourage one another and build each other up" (1 Thess. 5:11).

Positive reinforcement should be an obvious characteristic of your marriage.

Speak encouraging words to and about your spouse.

With Christ at the center of your home, His strength and supply will be your resources for keeping these scriptural commandments alive.

Developing Values for Your Home

Text: Eph. 4

The word *value* is defined by Webster's dictionary as "something (as a principle or quality) intrinsically valuable or desirable."[1]

Your home will be known by its value system.

Your personal values will influence the decisions, words, and actions in your home.

1. Why are values important? (vv. 2-3)

They guide us in decision-making.

They impact the way we treat others.

They influence our overall behavior.

They communicate our priorities.

2. How do I know if my values are good? (vv. 4-6)

Are they biblically based?

Can they be articulated to others?

Do they challenge me?

3. How can I walk worthy of my values? (vv. 11-16)

Walk in holiness. (vv. 22-29)

Walk in love. (5:1-2)

Walk in light. (vv. 8-9)

Qualities of a Christian Home

Text: 1 Pet. 4:8-10, NLT

Anyone can establish a home, but the qualities of a Christian home set it apart from all others. Today, you have the opportunity to begin building a Christian home—a home where Christ is honored, where His Word is truth, and where His characteristics are modeled.

There are some important qualities of a Christian home.

1. A Christian home constantly seeks after God.

Text: "But seek first his kingdom and his righteousness, and all these things will be given to you as well" (Matt. 6:33).

A Christian home seeks His will in every decision.

A Christian home seeks His way in every direction.

A Christian home seeks His power in every creation.

A Christian home seeks His peace in every reaction.

May you be God-seekers in every area of your life.

2. A Christian home puts others before self.

Text: "Be imitators of God, therefore, as dearly loved children and live a life of love, just as Christ loved us and gave himself up for us as a fragrant offering and sacrifice to God" (Eph. 5:1-2).

A Christian home would rather give than receive.

A Christian home would rather serve than be served.

A Christian home would rather restore than destroy.

May you love as Christ loved you.

3. A Christian home seeks to live a Spirit-filled life.

Text: "Do not get drunk on wine, which leads to debauchery. Instead, be filled with the Spirit" (Eph. 5:18).

A Christian home seeks to be surrendered to the Holy Spirit.

A Christian home seeks to be led by the Holy Spirit.

A Christian home seeks to be empowered by the Holy Spirit.

May you seek to live a lifestyle of holiness.

The Foundation of a Strong Family

Text: Josh. 24:15

1. The family is created by God.

Text: "The LORD God formed the man from the dust of the ground and breathed into his nostrils the breath of life, and the man became a living being" (Gen. 2:7).

God created us in His image. (Gen. 1:26-27)

God designed us for human companionship. (Gen. 2:18)

God established the original family unit. (Gen. 2:21-22)

2. The family is blessed by God.

Text: "For this reason a man will leave his father and mother and be united to his wife, and they will become one flesh" (Gen. 2:24).

Marriage fulfills God's purpose for the family. (Matt. 19:1, 4-6)

Procreation fulfills God's plan to populate the earth. (Gen. 1:28)

Nurture fulfills God's plan for training children. (1 Tim. 5:8)

3. The family must live by the principles of God.

Text: "Listen, my son, to your father's instruction and do not forsake your mother's teaching" (Prov. 1:8).

> The Bible requires mutual respect and submission in marriage. (Eph. 5:21)
>
> The Bible denotes the importance of sexual fulfillment in marriage. (1 Cor. 7:3-4)
>
> The Bible demands faithfulness to the marriage vows. (Heb. 13:4)

Be My Valentine Forever

Text: Gen. 2:20*b*-25; 29:26-30

(Note: Adam and Eve and Jacob and Rachel serve as the "valentines" for the text.)

February 14, better known as Valentine's Day, is "the traditional day on which lovers express their love for each other by sending Valentine's cards, presenting flowers, or offering confectionery."[2]

Modern-day Valentine's Day can be traced to the 1840s. "In the United States, the first mass-produced valentines of embossed paper lace were produced and sold after 1847 by Esther Howland of Worcester, Massachusetts."[3]

Marriage is the beginning of celebrating Valentine's Day for the rest of your life with someone you love.

1. Valentines forever starts with the God of forever.

God is the God of forever love.
God is the God of beginnings.
God is the God of connecting.
God is the God of hope.

2. **Valentines forever continues in the God of encouragement.**

   Encouragement to invest in each other
   Encouragement to learn from each other
   Encouragement to experience each other
   Encouragement to appreciate each other

3. **Valentines forever ends in the God of eternity.**

   A. Eternal values
      1. Faith
      2. Hope
      3. Charity
   B. Eternal priorities
      1. Time
      2. Sharing
      3. Exploration
   C. Eternal inspiration
      1. Vision
      2. Goals/dreams

If you wrote a valentine card for your spouse, what would it say?

Prescription for a Successful Marriage

Text: Gen. 2:18-25

Richard C. Cabot wrote, "Perhaps the greatest blessing in marriage is that it lasts so long. The years, like the varying interests of each year, combine to buttress and enrich each other. Out of many shared years, one life. In a series of temporary relationships, one misses the ripening, gathering, harvesting joys, and the deep, hard-won truths of marriage."[4]

1. Prescription One: Build on a genuine biblical foundation.

Build on the foundation of Christ first. Seek God in all things, including marriage.

Build on the foundation of unselfish agape love. The Greek word *agape* means a love that does not seek anything in return. It is an enduring, self-sacrificing, and others-centered love. It is a love that edifies, a love that serves, a love that cares.

Jerry White, in *The Power of Commitment*, wrote, "People fall in love, but they decide to stay in love. Emotions change like the weather, but love must be a determined commitment . . . We must commit to love in a self sacrificial way whether or not love is reciprocated."[5]

2. Prescription Two: Build a mutual admiration society.

Determine to focus on one another.

Determine to be positive with one another.

Determine to be proactive in committing to one another.

Determine to listen to one another.

Determine to be graceful in all situations with one another.

Continue to influence each other even in the midst of hurricane-like storms that hit every marriage. Don't pack your bags when the wind blows.

3. Prescription Three: Build a system of communication.

Speak from facts not feelings.

Speak out your opinions.

Speak with love.

Speak with understanding.

Speak about needs.

Gary Smalley, in *Making Love Last Forever,* writes, "The key to deep verbal intimacy is feeling safe to share our feelings and needs and sensing that our feelings and needs are valued by our mate."[6]

God loves each partner in a marriage and He counts both of them as special.

If we are willing, God will empower each one to maturity, love, forgiveness, compliments, and care.

The Dream of Love

Text: Song of Songs 2:8-13

The theme of the Book of the Song of Songs is the celebration of love. This very personal book is viewed by many biblical scholars as a love poem between King Solomon and his bride.

1. The excitement of love. (vv. 8-9)

   A lover's companionship is sharing conversation and thoughts together.

   A lover's companionship is hearing each other.

   A lover's companionship is embracing lives and knowing that all is right with the world.

   A lover's companionship is exhilarating more than anyone else's.

2. The invitation of love. (v. 10)

   The invitation includes acceptance.
   The invitation includes togetherness.
   The invitation includes wholeness.
   The invitation includes happiness.

3. The life of love. (v. 11-13)

   The life of openness to one another
   The life of enjoyment with one another
   The life of opportunities with each other
   The life of growing with each other

The Foundation of a Strong Marriage

Text: Gen. 2:18-25

The Garden of Eden provided Adam with all that he really needed—a terrific place to live, a super setting for fun, a wonderful walking path, and an interesting work environment. As interesting and fun as this was, something was missing from Adam's life. God, who knows our hearts the best, introduced Eve to Adam and his search was over!

Throughout this scripture, four thoughts produce the foundation for a strong marriage.

1. Change (v. 24a)

Change of preference
Change of pattern
Change of priority
Change of perspective

The leaving may seem not to apply. You've both left your parents' homes and established your own independence. But there is another level of leaving that is considerably more challenging. It is when you begin to leave behind your old habits of relating to people. It's the question of who you turn to for emotional support, and even for fun. Are you learning to turn to one another first? Friends and family are great. We need them. They have helped to shape you into the persons you are . . . You won't ever stop loving these people and enjoying their company. But how you relate to them will change, for your primary loyalty is to each other now. You are leaving behind the patterns of your past lives to build this new life together."[7]

2. **Permanence (v. 24*b*)**

A. Home
Finances
Jobs
Physical belongings

B. Outlook
Dreams
Hopes
Goals

C. Future
Togetherness
Children
Strength

3. **Intimacy (v. 25)**

Intimacy leads to physical unity.
Intimacy leads to emotional unity.
Intimacy leads to harmonious unity.
Intimacy leads to spiritual unity.

Intimacy is teamwork at its very best. We won't always be physically, emotionally, mentally, or spiritually in sync, but there will be a desire to ask what the other needs before thinking of oneself.

This will take a lifetime to achieve and there will be many failures along the journey, but it will be worked on continuously.

As Cheryl Rohret writes, "When each of you is giving 100 percent to the other, watch out! That is when rockets flare and love really blossoms!"[8]

What Is Love?

Text: 1 Cor. 13

David and Teresa Ferguson once said, "All marriages could use more of God, more of His Word, and more Christ-like attitudes that put each other first. And if we are to achieve a greater oneness and deeper intimacy in our marital relationship these things need to exist."[9]

Paul writes in 1 Corinthians that love is a reawakening of relationship. It teaches us what love is and how it should relate to your spouse.

1. Love is patient and kind. (v. 4*a*)

It understands when the day has been long.
It understands when a smile is needed.
It understands when we need a confirming word.
It understands when praise is appreciated.

"He that is slow to wrath is of great understanding" (Prov. 14:29).
"The patient in spirit is better than the proud in spirit" (Eccles. 7:8).
"Be kind and compassionate to one another, tenderhearted, forgiving each other, just as in Christ God forgave you" (Eph. 4:32).

2. Love is truth personified. (v. 6)

Truth challenges the heart.
Truth challenges the mind.
Truth challenges fear.
Truth challenges falsehood.

"You shall know the truth, and the truth shall make you free" (John 8:32).

"Truth is the radiant manifestation of reality."[10]

"The stream of truth flows through its channels of mistakes."[11]

3. Love persists forever. (v. 8)

Love persists through hardships.
Love persists through heartbreaks.
Love persists through nurture.
Love persists through life.

"Hatred stirs up dissension, but love covers over all wrongs" (Prov. 10:12).

"I will get up now and go about the city, through its streets and squares; I will search for the one my heart loves" (Song of Songs 3:2).

"Where there is no extravagance there is no love, and where there is no love there is no understanding."[12]

Scripture Readings

God created man in his own image, in the image of God he created him; male and female he created them. God blessed them and said to them, "Be fruitful and increase in number; fill the earth and subdue it. Rule over the fish of the sea and the birds of the air and over every living creature that moves on the ground" *(Gen. 1:27-28).*

The Lord God said, "It is not good for the man to be alone. I will make a helper suitable for him." Now the Lord God had formed out of the ground all the beasts of the field and all the birds of the air. He brought them to the man to see what he would name them; and whatever the man called each living creature, that was its name. So the man gave names to all the livestock, the birds of the air and all the beasts of the field. But for Adam no suitable helper was found. So the Lord God caused the man to fall into a deep sleep; and while he was sleeping, he took one of the man's ribs and closed up the place with flesh. Then the Lord God made a woman from the rib he had taken out of the man, and he brought her to the man.

The man said, "This is now bone of my bones and flesh of my flesh; she shall be called 'woman,' for she was taken out of man." For this reason a man will leave his father and mother and be united to his wife, and they will become one flesh *(Gen. 2:18-24)*.

He who finds a wife finds what is good and receives favor from the LORD *(Prov. 18:22)*.

From everlasting to everlasting the LORD's love is with those who fear him, and his righteousness with their children's children—with those who keep his covenant and remember to obey his precepts *(Ps. 103:17-18)*.

Do not forget my teaching, but keep my commands in your heart, for they will prolong your life many years and bring you prosperity. Let love and faithfulness never leave you; bind them around your neck, write them on the tablet of your heart. Then you will win favor and a good name in the sight of God and man. Trust in the LORD with all your heart and lean not on your own understanding; in all your ways acknowledge him, and he will make your paths straight *(Prov. 3:1-6)*.

Love and faithfulness keep a king safe; through love his throne is made secure *(Prov. 20:28)*.

He who pursues righteousness and love finds life, prosperity and honor *(Prov. 21:21)*.

Many waters cannot quench love; rivers cannot wash it away. If one were to give all the wealth of his house for love, it would be utterly scorned *(Song of Songs 8:7)*.

Two are better than one, because they have a good return for their work *(Eccles. 4:9)*.

"Haven't you read," he replied, "that at the beginning the Creator 'made them male and female,' and said, 'For this reason a man will leave his father and mother and be united to his wife, and the two will become one flesh'? So they are no longer two, but one. Therefore what God has joined together, let man not separate" *(Matt. 19:4-6)*.

So now I am giving you a new commandment: Love each other. Just as I have loved you, you should love each other. Your love for one another will prove to the world that you are my disciples *(John 13:34-35, NLT)*.

My command is this: Love each other as I have loved you *(John 15:12)*.

If I speak in the tongues of men and of angels, but have not love, I am only a resounding gong or a clanging cymbal. If I have the gift of prophecy and can fathom all mysteries and all knowledge, and if I have a faith that can move mountains, but have not love, I am nothing. If I give all I possess to the poor and surrender my body to the flames, but have not love, I gain nothing. Love is patient, love is kind. It does not envy, it does not boast, it is not proud. It is not rude, it is not self-seeking, it is not easily angered, it keeps no record of wrongs. Love does not delight in evil but rejoices with the truth. It always protects, always trusts, always hopes, always perseveres. Love never fails. But where there are prophecies, they will cease; where there are tongues, they will be stilled; where there is knowledge, it will pass away. For we know in part and we prophesy in part, but when perfection comes, the imperfect disappears. When I was a child, I talked like a child, I thought like a child, I reasoned like a child. When I became a man, I put childish ways behind me. Now we see but a poor reflection as in a mirror; then we shall see face to face. Now I know in part; then I shall know fully, even as I am fully known. And now these three remain: faith, hope and love. But the greatest of these is love *(1 Cor. 13)*.

The wife's body does not belong to her alone but also to her husband. In the same way, the husband's body does not belong to him alone but also to his wife *(1 Cor. 7:4)*.

But the fruit of the Spirit is love, joy, peace, patience, kindness, goodness, faithfulness, gentleness and self-control. Against such things there is no law. Those who belong to Christ Jesus have crucified the sinful nature with its passions and desires. Since we live by the Spirit, let us keep in step with the Spirit *(Gal. 5:22-25)*.

I urge you to live a life worthy of the calling you have received. Be completely humble and gentle; be patient, bearing with one another in love. Make every effort to keep the unity of the Spirit through the bond of peace *(Eph. 4:1-3)*.

Submit to one another out of reverence for Christ. Wives, submit to your husbands as to the Lord. For the husband is the head of the wife as Christ is the head of the church, his body, of which he is the Savior. Now as the church submits to Christ, so also wives should submit to their husbands in everything. Husbands, love your wives, just as Christ loved the church and gave himself up for her to make her holy, cleansing her by the washing with water through the word, and to present her to himself as a radiant church, without stain or wrinkle or any other blemish, but holy and blameless. In this same way, husbands ought to love their wives as their own bodies *(Eph. 5:21-28)*.

Therefore, as God's chosen people, holy and dearly loved, clothe yourselves with compassion, kindness, humility, gentleness and patience. Bear with each other and forgive whatever grievances you may have against one another. Forgive as the Lord forgave you. And over all these virtues put on love, which binds them all together in perfect unity *(Col. 3:12-14)*.

Marriage should be honored by all, and the marriage bed kept pure, for God will judge the adulterer and all the sexually immoral *(Heb. 13:4)*.

Everyone should be quick to listen, slow to speak and slow to become angry, for man's anger does not bring about the righteous life that God desires *(James 1:19-20)*.

Dear children, let us not love with words or tongue but with actions and in truth *(1 John 3:18)*.

Benedictions

May the grace of the Lord Jesus Christ, and the love of God, and the fellowship of the Holy Spirit be with all of you. Amen *(2 Cor. 13:14)*.

The Lord bless you and keep you; the Lord make his face to shine upon you, and be gracious to you; the Lord lift up his countenance upon you, and give you peace. Amen *(Num. 6:24-26, NKJV)*.

May the God who gives endurance and encouragement give you a spirit of unity as you follow Christ Jesus, so that with one heart you may glorify the God and Father of our Lord Jesus Christ. Amen *(Rom. 15:4-6)*.

Now unto him that is able to do exceeding abundantly above all that we ask or think, according to the power that worketh in us, unto him be glory in the Church by Christ Jesus throughout all ages. Amen *(Eph. 3:20, KJV)*.

To the only God our Savior be glory, majesty, power, and authority, through Christ our Lord, before all ages, now and forevermore. Amen *(Jude 1:25)*.

And now, I commend you to God, and to the word of his grace, which is able to build you up and to give you an inheritance among all them who are sanctified. Amen *(Acts 20:32, KJV)*.

Grace and peace to you from God our Father and the Lord Jesus Christ. Amen *(1 Cor. 1:3)*.

Appendixes

Appendix A

Wedding Application
Trinity Church of the Nazarene
7301 South Walker Avenue
Oklahoma City, OK 73139
Phone: 405-632-3307

Date of wedding _____ Time _____ Location _____

Name of Bride:

Last _____ Middle _____ First _____

Address _____

City _____ State _____ Zip _____

Tel: Home _____ Cell _____

Age _____

Parents' names _____

Single ___ Widowed ___ Divorced ____

Home church _____

Church member? ____

Name of Groom:

Last _____ Middle _____ First _____

Address _____

City _____ State _____ Zip _____

Tel: Home _____ Cell _____

Age _____

Parents' names _____

Single ___ Widowed ___ Divorced ____

Church attend _____

Church member? ____

Bride's Attendants	Groom's Attendants
_____	_____
_____	_____
_____	_____
_____	_____
_____	_____

Minister(s)

Name _____ Tel _____

Name _____ Tel _____

Wedding vows _____

Date of rehearsal _____ Time _____

Rehearsal dinner location _____ Time _____

Do you want the minister(s) to attend the rehearsal dinner? _____

Note: Please bring certificate of marriage license to the wedding rehearsal.

Wedding coordinator _____ Tel _____

Organist/piano/keyboards _____ Tel _____

Other:

Music _____

Soundtrack (CD _____ Other _____)

Video/PowerPoint _____ If so, length _____

Sound technician _____ Tel _____

Video technician _____ Tel _____

Photographer _____ Tel _____

Videographer _____ Tel _____

Photo/video session before the ceremony _____

Photo/video session following _____

Florist _____ Tel _____

Delivery date/time _____

Reception location _____

Reception caterer _____ Tel _____

Reception setup date/time _____

Person responsible for checking the building following the reception _____

Changing rooms needed _____

Nursery attendants _____

Detail arrangement of tables and chairs:

Arrangement for sound/video at the reception:

Have you read the Building Use Policy? _____

Will you comply with the Building Use Policy? _____

Signed _____ Date _____

FOR OFFICE USE ONLY

Deposit submitted _____ Date _____ Amount _____

Wedding fees submitted _____ Date _____ Amount _____

Refund mailed _____ Date _____ Amount _____

Contact person _____ Tel _____

Appendix B (Sample)

Wedding Showers
Trinity Church of the Nazarene
7301 South Walker Avenue
Oklahoma City, OK 73139
Phone: 405-632-3307

Trinity Church of the Nazarene provides wedding showers for the first wedding of church members. The Women's Ministries director will choose a coordinator that will plan and coordinate wedding showers.

If the wedding is a second marriage or the individuals are not members of Trinity Church, then the Sunday School class or ministry group will have the opportunity to sponsor the shower. These are not funded by the church.

Guidelines for the Coordinator

1. Contact the bride and groom as soon as possible and ask what kind of shower they prefer. The coordinator will help the person decide if a home or church shower should be selected. Church showers are usually held on Sunday evenings or during the fellowship time on Sunday mornings. Please check with the church office to select a date and time, and to make sure it gets on the calendar and into the bulletin.

2. Recruit a team to help with the shower. Duties will include: setup, serving, cleanup, washing tablecloths, etc. Table and chair

setups are to be arranged through the church facility manager at least two weeks prior to the shower.

3. If the shower is to be held in a home, the bride and groom should have an idea of friends who will want to serve as hostesses, etc. The coordinator will work with those individuals to plan the shower. Trinity reimburses up to $100 for expenses of the shower. This includes cake, punch, napkins, cups, etc.

4. If the shower is to be held at the church, the coordinator will plan and purchase items for the shower. Servers can be selected by the coordinator with input from the bride and groom. Trinity reimburses up to $100 for expenses of the shower. This includes cake, punch, napkins, cups, etc.

5. A full sheet cake usually serves one hundred guests and a half sheet serves fifty. Check with the bride and groom to see which colors are being used in the wedding and select accordingly for the shower cake(s).

6. Receipts will be turned in for each shower on the green sheets. These are located in the workroom of the church office. The discipleship team leader will need to approve the green sheets. The Women's Ministries director will explain the procedure to the wedding shower coordinator.

7. Tablecloths and skirts for the tables are in the storage room near Buchanan Hall. Following the wedding shower, please make sure the tablecloths are washed and returned ASAP. There are also decorations in the storage room that can be used.

8. Decorated gift tables are used with three chairs for the bride, groom, and the recorder to sit at as they open gifts. Do not begin to clean up until all gifts have been opened. Have plenty of helpers to clean up when the shower is officially over. Trash bags are located in the janitor's closet.

Appendix C

Building Use Policy

Trinity Church of the Nazarene
7301 South Walker Avenue
Oklahoma City, OK 73139
Phone: 405-632-3307

Bride's Name _____ Telephone No _____
Groom's Name _____ Telephone No _____
Wedding Date _____ Time _____

Building Use Policy for Weddings

Wedding—Active Church Member or Regular Attendee

	FEES	PAID	DUE
Wedding and Reception Total	$400	$____	$____
(Down payment to reserve date is included in total amount—see Guideline 1)	$100	$____	
TOTAL FEES:	$400	$____	$____
BALANCE DUE:		$____	

(Payable to the church office thirty days prior to wedding date.)

Fees cover the services of facility coordinator for weddings, sound technician, and custodians; they are not rental fees for the church facility.

Guidelines

1. A $100 down payment of the total fees must be received before the date is reserved on the church calendar. Make checks payable to **Trinity Church of the Nazarene,** mark for wedding, and bring or mail to the church office.

2. Food and drink must be limited to the fellowship hall.

3. Alcohol, drugs, smoking, and dancing are forbidden anywhere on church property. Birdseed may be used outside the building. No rice or bubbles inside the building, please!

4. The church property should be left in the same condition it is found.

5. Specific guidelines regarding building access dates and times, rooms, available equipment, and furniture movement will be provided by the facility coordinator for weddings upon request.

6. The facility coordinator for weddings *must be involved for consultation and assistance in planning and directing your wedding,* even if you use a personal wedding consultant.

7. There will be no Saturday weddings later than 3 P.M.

8. If an outside minister is to conduct or share in the ceremony, approval by the senior pastor is needed.

9. Our pastors require four premarital counseling sessions. These must be completed *at least* two weeks prior to the wedding date. Appointments may be arranged through the church office pastoral staff. Either the bride or groom or parent must be an active member or regular attendee of the church.

10. Arrangements for facility decorating must be made through the facility coordinator for weddings.

I have read and understand that this is a facility designed for worship. I agree to comply with the above guidelines. If I am unable to follow these guidelines, I understand the church has the right to cancel my wedding at this facility.

Signed _____ Date _____

Appendix D

Wedding Checklist

Trinity Church of the Nazarene
7301 South Walker Avenue
Oklahoma City, OK 73139
Phone: 405-632-3307

Date _____ Time _____

Officiating/Coordinating

___ Minister(s)
___ Wedding coordinator
___ Wedding license
___ Counseling appointments
___ Vows
___ Minister(s) attire
___ Honorarium
___ Announcement for publications

Wedding Site

___ Reservation
___ Fees
___ Setup instructions
___ Dressing rooms
___ Dressing room location
___ Dressing room amenities

Rehearsal and Reception

___ Rehearsal/wedding instructions
___ Schedule (arrival time)
___ Rehearsal dinner
___ Rehearsal dinner guests
___ Reception location
___ Reception menu
___ Reception caterer
___ Reception program
___ Reception decorations
___ Reception sound system
___ Reception special lighting

___ Reception personnel/staffing
___ Reception hosts
___ Reception gift opening
___ Custodian(s)
___ Setup times

Wedding Party (Bride)

___ Family seating
___ Maid/matron of honor
___ Bridesmaids
___ Flower girl
___ Rings
___ Ring bearer
___ Ring pillow
___ Guestbook/stand
___ Hostess
___ Attendant/assistant
___ Bridal attendant gifts
___ Gifts opening/records

Wedding Party (Groom)

___ Family seating
___ Best man
___ Ushers
___ Rings
___ Rehearsal dinner site
___ Rehearsal dinner menu
___ Rehearsal dinner payments
___ Gifts presentations

Wedding
- ___ Photographer(s)
- ___ Photography instructions
- ___ Videographer(s)
- ___ Video recording
- ___ Sound technician
- ___ Audio recording
- ___ Microphone placement
- ___ Audiovisual equipment
- ___ Lighting
- ___ Audiovisual presentations (PowerPoint, video, audio)
- ___ Musicians
- ___ Soloist(s)
- ___ Music
- ___ Soundtrack

- ___ Florist
- ___ Flowers
- ___ Rings
- ___ Candelabra
- ___ Candle lighting
- ___ Unity candle
- ___ Reserved seating
- ___ Communion elements
- ___ Kneeling bench
- ___ Aisle runner

Post Wedding
- ___ Receiving line
- ___ Photos
- ___ Reception cleanup

Appendix E

Wedding Ceremony Checklist

Trinity Church of the Nazarene
7301 South Walker Avenue
Oklahoma City, OK 73139
Phone: 405-632-3307

Date _____ Time _____

Prelude

Start time _____

Musicians _____

Music list

_____

_____

_____

_____

_____

_____

_____

_____

Seating of Family

Time _____

Groom's family members: Ushers(s) _____

Mother/father of groom: Usher _____

Groom's grandparents: Usher _____

Bride's family members: Usher(s) _____

Bride's grandparents: Usher _____

Mother of the bride: Usher _____

Candle Lighting

Name(s) _____

Music

Name _____ Song _____

Accompaniment _____

Bridal Procession

Minister(s)

Groom

Maid/matron of honor _____ Best man _____

Bride's Attendants	Groom's Attendants
_____	_____
_____	_____
_____	_____
_____	_____
_____	_____

Entrance of Flower Girl/Ring Bearer

Entrance of the Bride

Music

    Name _____ Song _____

    Accompaniment _____

Wedding Vows (including unity candle and/or Communion)

(Recognitions, e.g., giving of roses)

Introduction of Couple

Recessional

    Music _____

Receiving Line

    Location _____

    Names (L-R)

_____	_____
_____	_____
_____	_____
_____	_____
_____	_____

Appendix F

Seven Ways to Avoid the Wedding Day Blues

W—Welcome advice from a wedding coordinator. Experienced counsel doesn't cost; it pays.

E—Enjoy the process. Treat wedding details as ways to express your love.

D—Don't wait until the last moment. Planning ahead helps to alleviate anxiety and irritations.

D—Discipline yourself against overspending; set and practice budget guidelines.

I—Invite married friends to recommend hired services, such as musicians, sound experts, videographers, caterers, or decorators.

N—Never take sole ownership of the wedding; weddings are for couples.

G—Give instructions to the wedding participants. Don't assume anything.

Appendix G
Online Resources

Quotes and Ceremonies

en.thinkexist.com/quotes/top
www.bartleby.com
www.christianquotes.org
www.foreverwed.com
www.myweddingvows.com
www.quotationspage.com
www.quotegarden.com
www.quoteland.com

Articles/Videos/Downloads

www.christianity.com
www.crosswalk.com
www.focusonthefamily.com
www.gospel.com/ministries
www.loveandrespect.com
www.realrelationships.com
www.smalleyonline.com
www.winningathome.com

Books and Other Resources

www.nph.com
www.stantoler.com
www.wesleyan.org/wph/

Notes

1. *Merriam-Webster Online Dictionary,* s.v. "Value," <http://www.merriam-webster.com/dictionary/value> (accessed October 15, 2008).

2. Wikipedia contributors, "Valentine's Day," *Wikipedia, The Free Encyclopedia,* <http://en.wikipedia.org/w/index.php?title=Valentine%27s_Day&oldid=244025041> (accessed October 17, 2008).

3. Ibid.

4. ScarabBooks.com, "The Greatest Blessing in Marriage," <http://scarabbooks.com/uk/quoteaday/80/the-greatest-blessing-in-marriage/> (accessed October 16, 2008).

5. Jerry White, *The Power of Commitment* (Colorado Springs: NavPress, 1985), 88.

6. Gary Smalley, *Making Love Last Forever,* workbook ed. (Nashville: Thomas Nelson Publishers, 1997), 142.

7. Derl Keefer and Cheryl Rohret, *Wedding Sermons and Marriage Ceremonies* (Lima, Ohio: CSS Publishing Co., 2000), 53.

8. Albert M. Wells, Jr., *Inspiring Quotations* (Nashville: Thomas Nelson Publishers, 1988), 53-54.

9. David and Teresa Ferguson, *More Than Married* (Nashville: Thomas Nelson Publishers, 2000), 5-6.

10. Simone Weil, *The Need for Roots,* 2nd ed. (New York: Routledge, 2001), 61.

11. Rabinranath Tagore, *Stray Birds* (New York: The Macmillan Company, 1916), 98.

12. Oscar Wilde, quoted in *Oscar Wilde* by Richard Ellmann (New York: Vintage, 1988), 39.